Design Thinking

Design Thinking is a set of strategic and creative processes and principles used in the planning and creation of products and solutions to human-centered design problems.

With design and innovation being two key driving principles, this series focuses on, but not limited to, the following areas and topics:

- User Interface (UI) and User Experience (UX) Design

- Psychology of Design

- Human-Computer Interaction (HCI)

- Ergonomic Design

- Product Development and Management

- Virtual and Mixed Reality (VR/XR)

- User-Centered Built Environments and Smart Homes

- Accessibility, Sustainability and Environmental Design

- Learning and Instructional Design

- Strategy and best practices

This series publishes books aimed at designers, developers, storytellers and problem-solvers in industry to help them understand current developments and best practices at the cutting edge of creativity, to invent new paradigms and solutions, and challenge Creatives to push boundaries to design bigger and better than before.

More information about this series at https://www.springer.com/series/15933

Crafting Docs for Success

An End-to-End Approach to Developer Documentation

Diana Lakatos

Apress®

Crafting Docs for Success: An End-to-End Approach to Developer Documentation

Diana Lakatos
Szeged, Hungary

ISBN-13 (pbk): 978-1-4842-9593-9 ISBN-13 (electronic): 978-1-4842-9594-6
https://doi.org/10.1007/978-1-4842-9594-6

Managing Director, Apress Media LLC: Welmoed Spahr
Acquisitions Editor: James Robinson-Prior
Development Editor: Jim Markham
Editorial Assistant: Gryffin Winkler

Cover image designed by Isaac Soler at eStudioCalamar

Distributed to the book trade worldwide by Springer Science+Business Media New York, 1 New York Plaza, 1 FDR Dr, New York, NY 10004. Phone 1-800-SPRINGER, fax (201) 348-4505, e-mail orders-ny@springer-sbm.com, or visit www.springeronline.com. Apress Media, LLC is a California LLC and the sole member (owner) is Springer Science + Business Media Finance Inc (SSBM Finance Inc). SSBM Finance Inc is a **Delaware** corporation.

For information on translations, please e-mail booktranslations@springernature.com; for reprint, paperback, or audio rights, please e-mail bookpermissions@springernature.com.

Apress titles may be purchased in bulk for academic, corporate, or promotional use. eBook versions and licenses are also available for most titles. For more information, reference our Print and eBook Bulk Sales web page at http://www.apress.com/bulk-sales.

Any source code or other supplementary material referenced by the author in this book is available to readers on the Github repository. For more detailed information, please visit https://www.apress.com/gp/services/source-code.

Paper in this product is recyclable

Table of Contents

About the Author

 **Diana Lakatos** is an experienced Developer Documentation Specialist dedicated to creating high-quality resources for developers. She has played an instrumental role in the development of the multiple award-winning platformOS Developer Portal and manages all phases of the editorial workflow, creates templates, incorporates best practices, and writes, edits, and reviews content. She spoke about various aspects of building world-class developer docs at conferences like Write the Docs, tcworld, DevRelCon, and API The Docs.

About the Technical Reviewer

**Anne Gentle** is the Developer Experience Manager for developer advocacy, API documentation, and API quality assessments within developer relations and strategy at Cisco. With her teams of experts, she is responsible for developer tools for API design, developer documentation, and developer tutorials, including infrastructure integration and interactivity. Before her time at Cisco, Anne led large open-source communities in API documentation efforts and blazed trails supporting women in technology through internship programs like Outreachy. Anne was a Principal Engineer at Rackspace, serving on the OpenStack Technical Committee while advocating for cloud API users.

Anne wrote a book, *Docs Like Code*, to demonstrate developer tools and workflows like GitHub and automated publishing and code integration applied in the technical writing world. Anne proudly serves on the Workforce Advisory Committee at Austin Community College, pushing the field toward future API and developer documentation opportunities. In collaboration with the Inclusive Future Action Office at Cisco, Anne works with engineering teams to eliminate biased language in code and content.

Acknowledgments

I'd like to extend my appreciation to everyone who has been a part of this journey and contributed to the creation of this book.

First and foremost, I owe a heartfelt thank you to my family. Your love and support mean the world to me.

I am immensely thankful to Gyöngy Gora, a remarkably talented Senior UI Designer and Design System Specialist, for creating the visually engaging illustrations in the book.

I wish to express my gratitude to Kata Nagygyörgy, whose expertise in UX research has significantly enriched the content of this book.

Special thanks go to Péter Almási, a seasoned Senior Frontend Engineer, whose extensive experience greatly informed the technical aspects of the book.

A tremendous thank you goes to Anne Gentle, who meticulously reviewed the content of the book. Your precision and profound knowledge in the field have played a crucial role in ensuring the accuracy of this work.

I want to express my thanks to the platformOS team, with whom I had the privilege of building the platformOS Documentation. The collective knowledge and experiences we amassed have greatly shaped this book.

A big thank you to the Write the Docs community for your ongoing support, shared wisdom, and inspiring passion for creating quality documentation.

Finally, I want to express my appreciation to you, the readers. I hope the insights, strategies, and experiences shared within these pages contribute to your knowledge and success in the field of developer documentation.

Introduction

In 2018, I joined the platformOS team to establish documentation processes and build the developer portal for their model-based application development platform, targeting front-end developers and site builders.

We could essentially start from scratch: some content already existed (files in a GitHub repository written by developers), but there was no documentation site. It was the perfect time for me to join, as it provided us with the opportunity to develop a solid foundation to build upon.

As you can probably imagine, this felt like an overwhelming undertaking. I was the sole writer and documentation specialist in a team of 25 people, mostly developers, all working remotely. As our first move, we invited a UX researcher – from Chapter 2, "Foundations," onward, you'll understand why her involvement was essential. We used all the resources we could find: our previous experience working on developer portals, articles, courses, webinars, conference talks. There were a lot of excellent learning materials scattered all over the Internet (which I will share with you), but we had to figure out what to use and how to apply it to our project on our own. It was a lengthy process, and although it was overall a very rewarding experience, having a framework to follow and adjust as needed would have been greatly helpful. That's what this book aims to provide: a blueprint for building successful developer documentation, where I share our experience, along with practical, usable templates, workflows, and tools.

We're still a small remote team, but now we have a world-class developer portal that has become one of the most important assets for our community and business. Here's how you can craft docs for developer success, too.

CHAPTER 1

Approaches

Even if you are starting something from scratch, you probably don't have to start from zero: there is a good chance that other people have worked on something similar before, or came up with processes and solutions that you can apply to your project. The challenge is finding the approaches that would work for you.

This chapter explains approaches you can follow, why and how you can use them, and why they can be beneficial for any documentation project:

- Documentation as a product

- Design Thinking

- Docs as Code

- Community-driven documentation

- Content First

- Topic-based authoring and the Darwin Information Typing Architecture (DITA)

© Diana Lakatos 2023
D. Lakatos, *Crafting Docs for Success*, Design Thinking,
https://doi.org/10.1007/978-1-4842-9594-6_1

Note   I discuss these approaches because they have been immensely helpful for the whole process or specific aspects of building our developer documentation. Based on our experience, you can use and tweak them to create a good framework for most essential parts of your project, but you don't have to stop there. Keep up with relevant research, books, and conferences; be an active member of communities where documentarians, developers, developer relations professionals, and UX practitioners connect; and stay on the lookout for other approaches that might inspire you.

Documentation As a Product

Your developer documentation is naturally linked to the product it documents, but considering the crucial role it plays in the adoption, use, and marketing of your product, it should be considered a product in its own right.

Your developer documentation can become your most important asset in developer relations that fulfills a wide range of different functions:

- It should provide all the necessary information for developers to start working with your product as the key ingredient in your onboarding.

- It should be a reliable source for self-help and education.

- It should be a platform to keep your users informed on changes and plans through release notes, status reports, and various content updates.

- It can build trust and show your users how committed you are, how much you value their feedback as you shape the documentation to best fit their needs.

- It can help you maintain relationships with your users, build a community, and encourage collaboration.

- Documentation can work as an interactive tool between you and the developers using your product by making it possible for them to immediately share their thoughts and suggestions on the docs so that you can act on them quickly.

- It's also a marketing tool: many potential clients will find you through your developer portal. Decision-makers also check out your documentation to see the quality of support you provide.

- It can be a valuable resource for your support team who can in turn provide feedback about the documentation from direct communication with users.

- It can become the foundation for your developer education program, webinars, courses, certification programs, and so on.

Tip   You can use the preceding list as an outline for collecting your arguments if you need to convince stakeholders about the value developer documentation can bring to the business.

To be able to build documentation that excels in all these roles, you will need to think strategically about your docs. Explore how the documentation aligns with the broader vision for the product and the company. Ask questions about the problem the documentation is solving, who your users are and what they need, and how you measure success.

You and your company have to see your docs for what they really are: a complex product that needs attention, time, resources, and funding to be successful.

Design Thinking

Design Thinking is a human-centered iterative design process that consists of predefined steps you can follow to understand your users, reevaluate your assumptions, define or redefine problems, and create solution prototypes that you can test.

The origins of Design Thinking go back to the development of psychological studies on creativity and creativity techniques in the 1940s and 1950s, and the approach has been refined ever since to arrive at a state where it's now widely considered to be a generalizable approach to technical and social innovation.

Note   If you would like to learn more about the interesting history and other aspects of Design Thinking, I suggest you read *The Design Thinking Playbook*[1] by Michael Lewrick, Patrick Link, and Larry Leifer; select some books you're interested in from the Apress Design Thinking series[2]; or delve deeper into online articles on the topic, for example, by the Interaction Design Foundation[3].

---

[1]https://www.amazon.com/Design-Thinking-Playbook-Transformation-Businesses/dp/1119467470
[2]https://www.springer.com/series/15933
[3]https://www.interaction-design.org/

The Phases of the Design Thinking Process

The Design Thinking process has multiple phases. The number of phases sometimes varies between different schools, but the idea of a dynamic, iterative process is at the core of all models. This book describes the model consisting of five phases recommended by the Hasso Plattner Institute of Design at Stanford because it can be used efficiently for a developer documentation project.

- **Phase 1: Empathize**

  Develop a deep understanding of the challenge by setting aside your assumptions and gaining insights about your users through user research. Try to get rid of any preconceived ideas you have about the tasks your users want to accomplish, how they approach them, and what obstacles they may face. Listen and explore with an open mind, and be aware of your biases so that you don't focus on results that confirm them.

- **Phase 2: Define**

  Analyze the information you collected in the Empathize phase and describe the problem you want to solve. You can create personas – semi-fictional, archetypical users whose goals and characteristics represent the needs of larger user groups or target audience segments. Personas are one way to help you keep the process human-centered through all phases.

- **Phase 3: Ideate**

  Based on the knowledge from the previous phases, try to consider the problem from different points of view, brainstorm ideas, and identify innovative solutions.

- **Phase 4: Prototype**

  Experiment, and identify the best possible solution
  for each problem. Come up with cost-efficient ways to
  design scaled-down versions of your solutions that you
  can quickly develop, produce, adjust, or discard.

- **Phase 5: Test**

  Start a testing process that consists of short cycles to
  redefine or improve your solutions. You might gain
  more insights about your users or further problems
  might emerge, so you might need to return to previous
  phases and iterate.

Although you can use these phases as a step-by-step process, they
do not always have to be sequential, as the Design Thinking process is
iterative and nonlinear. You can work on phases in parallel, or repeat some
phases or cycles until you arrive at the required result. Figure 1-1 shows
the phases step by step and highlights some possible cycles of iteration.

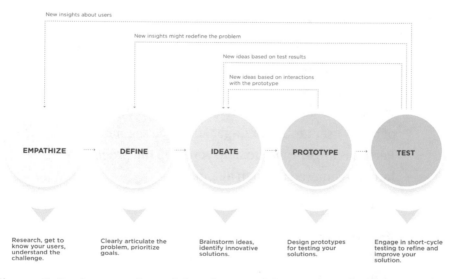

Figure 1-1. *An overview of the phases of the Design Thinking process*

Design Thinking in Your Developer Documentation Project

The Design Thinking process can be applied to the development of your developer documentation on multiple levels.

Whole Process

Following the phases of the Design Thinking approach step by step provides a great framework for documentation development. Table 1-1 shows how each phase can be mapped to specific tasks, which ensures that you are following a well-defined plan and can keep track of where you are in the process.

Table 1-1. *Mapping documentation development tasks to the phases of the Design Thinking process*

Design Thinking phase	Goal of the phase	Documentation development tasks
Empathize	Collect as much information about the project as possible, and develop a deep understanding of your users and the challenge.	Discovery phase, where you explore your audience, your documentation needs, and business needs of the stakeholders through in-depth interviews.
Define	Clearly articulate the problem you want to solve and prioritize the goals.	Define personas; create a content inventory. Identify challenges, pain points, and main goals.
Ideate	Brainstorm potential solutions; select and develop your solution.	Hold workshops, and share your ideas for content and features. Prioritize content needs.

(continued)

7

Table 1-1. (*continued*)

Design Thinking phase	Goal of the phase	Documentation development tasks
Prototype	Design prototypes to test all or part of your solution.	Create a sitemap, layouts, wireframes, and design. Start content production. Build an editorial workflow and a development workflow.
Test	Engage in a short-cycle testing process to refine and improve your solution.	Validate and test. Continuously improve features and content based on feedback from real users.

Figure 1-2 shows an overview of the phases of the Design Thinking process with the documentation development tasks added.

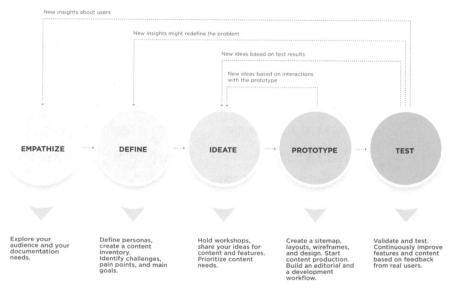

Figure 1-2. *Documentation development tasks in the Design Thinking process*

Note   The processes, methods, and activities described in Chapters 2–5 of this book can be mapped to the Design Thinking process as follows:

Chapter 2: Foundations – Empathize, Define, Ideate

Chapter 3: Editorial Workflow – Ideate, Prototype

Chapter 4: Content Production – Ideate, Prototype

Chapter 5: Implementation – Prototype, Test

Each Area of Focus

At the same time, each area you focus on can go through the same process. For example, when you develop your editorial workflow:

1. You get to know your target audience and **empathize** with their needs, problems, and obstacles.

2. You **define** what they need in an editorial workflow.

3. You **ideate**, brainstorm, and look for solutions that would fulfill their needs.

4. You design a **prototype** of your editorial workflow.

5. You **test** it with real users and adjust it; you can go back to reevaluating your target audience, redefine their needs, and ideate about solutions, too.

For a developer documentation project, we found that such an iterative approach works very well. It provides enough data to progress but leaves enough room for course correction and adjustment.

From the perspective of building developer documentation, the most important aspect of Design Thinking is **empathy for the user** - it should be the driving force behind everything you do. Practically, this means that you'll do a lot of research and go through a lot of iterations. You'll need a workflow that allows you to work with quick feedback rounds, deploy often, and improve features and content based on feedback from real users. Docs as Code fulfills all of these requirements and more.

Docs as Code

Docs as Code (also called Docs Like Code) refers to the approach of treating documentation development similarly to code development. This typically means

- Using the same or similar tools as development teams like version control, issue trackers, and solutions for continuous integration and continuous delivery.

- Following the same or similar workflows as development teams like review and approval processes. This can also include methodologies like agile project management practices.

In practice, this means that you

- Store the documentation source files in your version control system like git (e.g., on GitHub[4], GitLab[5], or Gerrit[6]). For writing and editing content, a lightweight markup language (like Markdown[7] or AsciiDoc[8]) is most often used.

- Review changes with reviewers collaborating in the version control system.

---

[4]https://github.com/
[5]https://about.gitlab.com/
[6]https://www.gerritcodereview.com/
[7]https://www.markdownguide.org/
[8]https://asciidoc.org/

- Build the documentation automatically. Docs as Code workflows often use a static site generator to build the docs.

- Publish the changes without much manual intervention through a CI/CD workflow (e.g., using Jenkins[9], Netlify[10], or GitHub Actions[11]). Automated tests help with quality assurance.

Note   Chapter 3, "Editorial Workflow," describes a Docs-as-Code workflow in detail, while Chapter 5, "Implementation," discusses options for the technical implementation. If you'd like to learn more about this approach, I suggest you read the book *Docs Like Code*[12] by Anne Gentle.

Docs as Code for Developer Documentation

Docs as Code is a great match for developer documentation projects because your main contributors, developers on your team and in your community, are already familiar with these workflows and tools. They don't need to learn new tools to start contributing to your docs, and they can follow a process they are comfortable with – this removes at least some barriers to entry while you can work on removing others like a lack of confidence in language or writing skills.

---

[9]https://www.jenkins.io/
[10]https://www.netlify.com/
[11]https://github.com/features/actions
[12]https://www.docslikecode.com/book

You can get inspired by the workflows and tools the engineering team works with to develop your documentation with the added benefit that they will be ready to jump in and use the same tools when you need them to contribute to the docs.

Docs as Code has its constraints, but fortunately, those are less pronounced when you are building developer documentation.

Although developers and technical writers will probably contribute the most content to your developer docs, **the workflow should also accommodate other contributors** like users in less technical roles, UX practitioners, or account and project managers. So you should find ways to simplify your Docs-as-Code workflow for them, for example, by choosing a readable markup language, providing support materials, or offering an online text editor.

Working in a Docs-as-Code environment **requires technical knowledge**, which means that your technical writers will need to be comfortable using the tools you chose. You'll have to consider how to manage updates: you want to be able to quickly update content on your documentation and do so as frequently as you'd like to. You have to build an editorial workflow that contributors will use, and test and tweak it to best fit their needs. You'll need engineering support to build and adjust your processes – which is easiest to achieve if your company's leadership understands the value that developer documentation brings to the business. If you're working with open source tools, you might be concerned about the longevity of those tools and will need to be aware of some alternative solutions in case the ones you are using are no longer maintained.

Docs-as-Code Benefits

If you are aware of the limits and address them while planning, building, and adjusting your workflow, Docs as Code offers some added benefits that might not be obvious at first.

If your team and community members are scattered across different time zones, you probably communicate asynchronously most of the time, meaning that when you send a message, you don't expect an immediate response. Docs as Code fully supports **asynchronous communication** because all contributors can review, comment, change something in the same repository at different times, and find all the changes and suggestions made by others. This also makes it easier to distribute work between different teams; for example, the UX team contributes an article to the documentation about the latest user research, and someone from the writer team reviews, edits, and merges it.

Contributors also have to be able to **control their own environments**, as docs have become mobile and cross-platform compatible. So it shouldn't matter what operating system you are using, or what your editor of choice is.

Docs as Code makes it easier to leverage the power of your community and **involve specialists** that you otherwise might not be able to involve. Especially if your documentation is open source, you can find contributors for topics and tasks that require specific knowledge, or test and improve the accessibility of your documentation with users from a wide range of abilities.

Docs as Code makes it possible to **decouple content from display**, which means that you can write content with basic formatting without worrying about what it would look like on the site. It also means that the structure of the content is well defined, so design updates are easier to do and your style will remain consistent.

The greatest achievement of Docs as Code above all the practical aspects discussed previously and all throughout this book is that it enables a culture where all contributors **feel ownership of documentation**. With the right support, it provides the technical foundations for an inclusive environment where everyone can contribute according to their specific skills and expertise to make your developer documentation as good as it can be.

Community-Driven Documentation

Your documentation plays a strategic role in the adoption and use of your product, so you should approach the development of your docs with a mindset that ensures that

- Your users get the most out of your documentation as early as possible

- You receive feedback as soon and as often as possible

- You never lose sight of your long-term goals

Knowing your target audience is key to great documentation, so being able to get to know your users and directly communicate with them is a huge advantage. You should aim to develop a good relationship with your community to be able to involve them in all phases of your documentation process starting from the very beginning, the discovery phase.

Involving your users early on in a dynamic and iterative process ensures that you **can test and validate all of your assumptions** and quickly modify anything if needed. This is a time and cost-efficient approach. Although you'll have to change code and content on your documentation site frequently, you won't run the risk of creating large chunks of work that have to be thrown away because they don't correspond to the needs of your users.

Constant collaboration also **builds trust**: if your process is completely transparent, your community can continuously follow what you're working on and how your docs evolve, and community members can be sure that their opinions are heard and acted upon.

Although the advantages of involving your community early on far outweigh the risks, be aware that it means that your users will encounter missing or partially done content, features that might not work as expected, navigation that might change multiple times, or topics that will be moved, removed, or completely rewritten. For all of this to work, you will need to communicate with your users clearly and frequently. Explain each change by referring to the research or feedback that prompted the change. When conducting user research, always communicate the goal clearly, and explain how the results will be used. Share your plans and ask your community if they align with their expectations.

Note   Upcoming chapters will delve into different aspects of getting to know and interacting with your users. Chapter 2, "Foundations," discusses ways for learning more about your target audience segments. Chapter 6, "Community," explores the many ways you can provide for your users to contribute and discusses the communication channels you can establish for engaging in constant communication with your community.

Content First

Content First is a design approach that **uses the content to define the layout and design** instead of using placeholder text and images throughout the prototyping phase and adding real content only during implementation. When you start designing with existing content (or templates) instead of dummy text, you can decide what design would make the most sense for it – instead of doing it the other way around where you have designs signed off before you start to produce any content, and then desperately try to come up with copy that you could pour into the design.

The goal of a documentation site is to **provide easily accessible, well-structured information for self-support and learning** that is written, edited, and structured in a way that best fits the user's needs. When building documentation, content is your top priority.

Once you have an understanding of your target audience, you can start exploring what types of content you'll create for them, and think about the display of the content only after that. This doesn't mean that you'll have to have all content written by the time you start designing, but you will have to know what types of content you'll need and have an idea about the structure and organization of your content early on (which you will then change many times over).

To establish the basic structure of your content and the most often used content types, you can get some inspiration from topic-based authoring and the Darwin Information Typing Architecture, usually referred to as DITA.

Topic-Based Authoring and DITA

Topic-based authoring or topic-based writing refers to the practice of **writing content in small, modular units** called topics that are stand-alone pieces of information that can be used for single sourcing, content reuse, or creating larger units of information.

A topic is the smallest possible chunk of information that is as self-contained as possible. You can provide continuity for prerequisite knowledge, references, or next steps as links to other topics. This is very useful in an environment like a developer documentation site where any topic could be the page the user has landed on (e.g., after a Google search).

Topic-based authoring works very well with a **minimalistic approach**. Users who try to learn or do something need guidance that is easy to follow and is not convoluted with information they don't need. Minimalism improves the quality and effectiveness of technical documentation, as it focuses on the user's goals, takes an action-oriented approach, eliminates fluff and unnecessary context, and improves findability. Edit each topic so that it includes the required amount of information for the user to accomplish a task or understand a concept – and nothing more. For procedural content, you can string together topics that describe each stand-alone action of that procedure.

This approach is extremely valuable when you have to update information. If the change concerns one task, you update the topic for that task, and every other topic that points to the updated topic will now lead users to the updated information. If you have to reorganize your content, you just have to change the ordering and grouping of topics instead of editing large chunks of content. Once you have defined your topic types and their structure, the approach helps keep writing consistent even with many contributors.

To define the topic types and their structure, you can get inspired by the Darwin Information Typing Architecture (DITA)[13]. Originally developed by IBM, then open-sourced and now maintained by the OASIS DITA Technical Committee, DITA is an open standard that defines **a set of document types for authoring and organizing topic-oriented information**.

The latest version of DITA (1.3) includes five topic types: task, concept, reference, glossary entry, and troubleshooting. All of these can be used for your developer documentation content, and you might define other content types, too. The three main content types – task, concept, reference – will cover most of the content in your docs.

- **Task:** Task topics are building blocks to provide procedural information. They describe how to accomplish a task through a series of steps and can also include context, links to prerequisites and next steps, and examples.

- **Concept:** Concept topics provide background information and other essential information that the user needs to know to understand a system, product, or solution. They can explain features and components, introduce technology, or outline a process.

---

[13]http://docs.oasis-open.org/dita/dita/v1.3/dita-v1.3-part0-overview.html

- **Reference:** Reference topics provide data to support performing a task and usually include information that is looked up rather than memorized. They are often displayed as lists or tables.

Note   Chapter 4, "Content Production," demonstrates how you can use topic-based authoring and topic types inspired by DITA to create templates for the most often used topic types.

Summary

This chapter gave you ideas for approaches you can leverage in your developer documentation project. Although the challenge is great, you can rely on well-defined and tested methodologies to

- Establish the mindset for everyone involved to consider developer documentation a product in its own right *(documentation as a product)*

- Follow an iterative process to understand your users, reevaluate your assumptions, define problems, and create solutions you can test *(Design Thinking)*

- Build a workflow that will serve your contributors and ensure a smooth process for frequent changes *(Docs as Code)*

- Involve your users early on and collaborate with them on all aspects of your docs *(community-driven documentation)*

- Start with your content structure and content types to base your layouts and designs on *(Content First)*

- Understand the structure of your content and the most often used content types *(topic-based authoring and DITA)*

You are now ready to start building the foundations.

CHAPTER 2

Foundations

Regardless of the current state of your developer documentation, whether you're starting from scratch, rebuilding or improving your existing documentation, or fine-tuning a well-functioning documentation site, you can only expect good results if you build on solid foundations. You have to achieve a deep understanding of the people who use your product and your docs and provide them with the tools they need to accomplish their goals.

The discovery phase is essential because it's where you build this solid foundation for all of the work to come. This chapter walks you through a procedural overview of the discovery phase, with detailed explanations for each step along with a practical demonstration of tools and methods with real-world examples.

Project Discovery

Building or improving developer documentation can be considered a project where all rules of project discovery apply: you collect and analyze information about your project to identify its vision, goals, and scope. Your goal with the project discovery is to roughly estimate what resources you will need and to make decisions based on real data as much as you can. You will still have some assumptions that you can later reevaluate and adjust, but you will gain an understanding of the project to start it with confidence.

© Diana Lakatos 2023
D. Lakatos, *Crafting Docs for Success*, Design Thinking,
https://doi.org/10.1007/978-1-4842-9594-6_2

During the project discovery, you:

- Figure out which team members, external contributors, and users to involve

- Get into the habit of doing a lot of research (and never stop)

- Establish a rough timeline and budget

- Plan next steps based on the information you collected

Throughout the whole process, you'll have to make sure that the documentation you are planning is:

- **Desirable:** Conduct various forms of user research to ensure that your solution fulfills user needs.

- **Viable:** Interview stakeholders to ensure that your solution corresponds to business needs.

- **Feasible:** Ensure that you have the resources, developer capacity, time, and technical background to build your solution.

Although all throughout this book I often encourage you to focus on user needs, you can't ignore the other two factors without risking the success of your whole project. You have to regularly communicate with your company leadership and team members in sales, marketing, account management, and product management to be aware of business needs and future plans to adjust your road map or change course in sync with company goals. To be able to implement and iterate on your documentation, you have to work closely with your development team to find technical solutions for your workflow and features and have the capacity and time to plan, develop, test, and iterate.

The first steps of the discovery process like the competitive analysis and initial user research rounds belong to the **Empathize** phase of the Design Thinking process.

User Research

Research is the fundamental way to collect the information you need and achieve an understanding of the people who use your product. For a developer documentation project, market research is usually not needed, as it's probably been done for your product already. User research, including a competitive analysis, will provide the most useful information, insights, and ideas. You should do user research at all stages of your documentation development process because there's always something useful to learn. Conducting research and analyzing data is a complex task, so I recommend having at least one UX researcher available to your developer documentation team (more on this in Chapter 9, "Team"). You will find that each research activity increases the quality of your documentation and the value it provides to your users.

User research helps you understand user expectations, behaviors, needs, and motivations through methodical, investigative approaches, therefore empowering you to provide the information and experience that best fits their needs.

You can collect different types of information through user research:

- **Attitudinal or behavioral:** The purpose of attitudinal research is to understand users' beliefs (what they say), while behavioral research seeks to understand users' actions (what they do).

- **Qualitative or quantitative:** Qualitative research answers how and when a certain phenomenon occurs by providing non-numerical information. Quantitative research is an investigation using statistical, mathematical, or computational techniques.

Before starting user research, always agree with your team on

- **Goals:** What's the purpose of this research, what are you trying to achieve, what insights will this research generate, and how will you use those insights?

- **Problems:** What is the problem you are trying to solve?

- **Assumptions:** What assumption or belief do you want to test and what do you need to validate or explore?

- **Information:** What do you need to know to be able to make a decision? Has anything been done related to this research already (e.g., other research or analysis)?

Once you have answered these questions, you need to specify what target audience segment you'd like to involve. Describe their roles, knowledge level, and any other relevant factor that will make it clear who you should invite to the user research.

Then, before jumping into organizing and conducting the research, define your **research success criteria**: What will make this research successful? What qualitative or quantitative information will you collect? What document would you like to create? What decision needs to be made based on the research results?

Based on all the information you collected, find a suitable research method.

User Research Methodologies

Different user research methodologies lend themselves to different stages of your documentation development cycle. For example, you can start the discovery with field and diary studies, user and stakeholder interviews, and continue your exploration by conducting workshops and exercises to build personas, identify tasks, and write user stories. When testing your prototype, you might do in-person or remote usability studies, and accessibility evaluations. Later, you might want to do some surveys and delve into analytics.

There are many user research methodologies to choose from. As a start, it's useful to be familiar with a couple of them:

- **Competitive analysis:** Compare strengths, weaknesses, features, flows, and the user experience of your competitors relative to your documentation plans based on user feedback.

- **Interviews:** Meet your users and people from sales, marketing, and company leadership to discuss in depth how the participant experiences the topic in question.

- **(Remote) Usability testing:** Usability testing involves asking potential or current users of a product or service to complete a set of tasks and then observing their behavior to determine the usability of the product or service.

  - **Moderated (remote) usability testing** allows you to conduct user research with participants in their natural work environment. Participants are observed and interacted with while they complete the tasks for the test. Moderated testing is best for complex tasks that do not have a structured sequence of steps or where more interaction and questioning will benefit testing.

- **Unmoderated (remote) usability studies** are designed to measure how satisfied a user is with the interface of your documentation. The idea is that participants will work through a task in their usual environment without a moderator present. They are shorter and less complex than moderated usability studies.

- **Card sorting:** A quantitative or qualitative method that asks users to organize items into groups and assign categories to each group. This method helps create or refine the information architecture of your documentation by exposing users' mental models.

- **Tree tests:** Tree tests are helpful in validating the information architecture. In a tree test, users are given a task and shown the top level of a site map. They are then asked to talk about where they would go to accomplish the task.

- **Surveys, questionnaires:** Questionnaires and surveys are an easy way to gather a large amount of information about a group. This quantitative data can help you to have a better understanding of specific topics that you can research further with other methods.

- **Analytics review:** Site analytics provide quantitative data about usage and identify possible flow breaks that you can test further in usability research.

Each research method has its own way of analyzing and synthesizing the results, but the goal is always to find patterns that emerge across participants, have a better understanding of related aspects, and gain insights into the underlying reasons for the different behaviors and answers. These insights are then utilized to shape the decisions about your documentation.

Tip   If you would like to get some more insights about user research methodologies, I recommend you to read *Universal Methods of Design – 125 Ways to Research Complex Problems, Develop Innovative Ideas, and Design Effective Solutions*[1] by Bella Martin and Bruce Hanington and *Just Enough Research*[2] by Erica Hall.

Once you have a rough idea of the vision, scope, and goals for your developer documentation, you can start building the foundation for your docs by following a series of different user research rounds aimed at collecting all the information you need to get to know your audience, figure out what content you need, and be able to outline a sitemap for your documentation site. The process described here is an example – feel free to experiment and customize it to your own documentation project.

Competitive Analysis

Starting to develop a documentation site or doing larger changes can seem daunting. Conducting some form of competitor research is a good way to ease yourself into the process while gaining useful insights and getting some cool ideas.

A competitive analysis can provide strategic insights into the features, flows, and user experience provided by your competitors.

---

[1] https://www.amazon.com/Universal-Methods-Design-Expanded-Revised/dp/1631597485
[2] https://abookapart.com/products/just-enough-research

Doing basic competitor research for developer documentation can be approached from different angles; let me share a couple that worked very well for us:

- Find your closest competitors. Discover and write up a list of products similar to yours that have a similar target audience. Examine their documentation in great detail. Find patterns for structure, language, navigation, and organization.

- Find great examples of developer documentation and take notes of what users like about them. Check out popular talks by respected documentation specialists, and explore the aspects they talked about on the documentation sites they showed as examples. Browse previous winners of awards aimed at recognizing documentation excellence like the DevPortal Awards[3], DevRel Awards[4], or UK Technical Communication Awards[5]. Different award categories help you determine what aspects the documentation sites were praised for, and judges' feedback usually gives you a detailed explanation of why the entry was recognized in the chosen category.

- Ask developers on your team or among your friends which documentation they like and why. Write up a list of products they mention.

---

[3]https://devportalawards.org/

[4]https://devrelawards.com/

[5]https://istc.org.uk/homepage/professional-development-and-recognition/uk-technical-communication-awards/

During a competitive analysis, you not only compare the strengths and weaknesses of your competitors and your planned offering but also gain insights based on user feedback. As a start, you can cover three to five competitors and analyze two to three flows from each. You can even test the flows of your competitors with real users. Based on the results, you can gain insights about the strengths and weaknesses of your documentation plans.

You might come back from the competitive analysis with vastly different feelings: You might get the impression that it's all too complex and you'll never make it. You might have seen such great solutions that you just want to jump in and copy them (which is fine as long as you validate and adjust them for your users). You might come back with a couple of good ideas but no way to know how to implement the whole thing.

Don't worry, you are building your documentation for *your* users, so you will have to get to know them and validate your assumptions anyway. Here's where user research will enter (and stay with you for the whole lifetime of your docs).

Target Audience

Regardless of what kind of content you write, you have to know who will read and use that content. Knowing your target audience ensures that you can address real user needs and gain an empathetic understanding of the problems they are trying to solve.

Developers

As you are working on developer documentation, you already know who your main target audience is: **developers**. This is an advantage you should use. Look for research papers, talks, and articles that explain how developers use documentation and gather all the knowledge you can about how they approach problems, what strategies they adopt to solve a task, or how much risk they take.

For a basic understanding of these aspects, I summarize the findings of the following research about the way developers approach problems:

- Clarke, S. (2007) What is an end user software engineer?[6] – Dagstuhl Seminar Proceedings, Schloss Dagstuhl - Leibniz-Zentrum für Informatik

- Watson, R. B. (2015) The effect of visual design and information content on readers' assessments of API reference topics[7] (doctoral dissertation)

- Meng, M., Steinhardt, S., Schubert, A. (2019) How Developers Use API Documentation: An Observation Study[8] – Communication Design Quarterly (January 29, 2019)

Tip   These research papers include a lot of useful information, so I recommend getting familiar with them in more depth.

Naturally, each individual developer is unique, and developer communities are diverse. Many developers might not fall into the categories described in these research papers. It's still invaluable to become familiar with the different patterns research has identified to look for and evaluate whether these patterns apply to your target audience.

---

[6]https://drops.dagstuhl.de/opus/volltexte/2007/1080/
[7]https://digital.lib.washington.edu/researchworks/handle/1773/33466
[8]https://www.researchgate.net/publication/335456576_How_developers_use_API_documentation_an_observation_study

Note You will also have to think about differences between native and non-native speakers, neurodiversity, and users with varying abilities. I will address these topics in Chapter 7, "Accessibility and Inclusion."

Clarke (2007) found that developers' approaches to coding and learning could be categorized into three groups: systematic, opportunistic, and pragmatic.

Systematic developers follow a defensive, top-down approach and take precautions. They learn about concepts and architecture and gain a deep understanding of the technology before they start to use it.

They read the documentation thoroughly and usually follow proposed processes and recommendations. They set up their development environment as instructed and use and modify example code.

Systematic developers feel accomplished when they write clean and elegant code to complete a task.

Opportunistic developers follow a bottom-up approach. They start coding immediately focusing on solving the problem at hand and only gather as much information as they need to work on the task.

They scan the documentation to find the information they need and are less likely to follow proposed processes. They might deviate from the recommended workflow or order of steps and usually search the Web in parallel with using the official documentation and coding.

Opportunistic developers are explorers who take pride in solving problems.

Pragmatic developers combine systematic and opportunistic approaches. They learn until they develop a sufficient understanding of the technology, but they don't delve deeper than needed for accomplishing the task.

They use the documentation and other resources to learn enough to start the task beforehand and then consult these resources again when they encounter an obstacle.

Pragmatic developers take delight in building robust applications.

Although each developer might have a characteristic approach, they might follow different approaches for different tasks, or under different circumstances. Regardless of the approach, as a bare minimum, they all need

- Conceptual information *(concept topics)*

- Procedural information *(task topics)*

- References *(reference topics)*

- Code examples

- Clear navigation

- Efficient search

The developers using your documentation also have different experience levels both regarding software development in general and regarding the skills needed to use your product. Your developer documentation will probably be used by technical people with various levels of programming skills like junior, midlevel, or senior, and with different areas of interest like back-end, front-end, or full-stack developers, site builders, or CTOs – including members of your own team.

You will have to evaluate the experience level of these target audience segments early and reevaluate it relatively often, as it has a great impact on your onboarding process, and the structure and content of your documentation. You will probably have to cater to different experience levels and different learning styles all throughout your docs.

Other Target Audience Segments

Learning more about developers and catering to their needs give you the right focus, but for your developer documentation to fulfill all its roles, you have to keep other target audience segments in mind as well.

People working in various **support** roles will consult your documentation to solve problems for their own users. Your documentation should also serve your own support team, and it should work both ways. Well-structured, topic-oriented documentation helps support teams share well-defined topics for specific questions, and in return, your support team can contribute to your docs by providing feedback and improvement suggestions, highlighting areas that need more attention, and producing content.

Product owners, **business analysts**, and **project managers** will visit your docs to evaluate if your solution would be a good fit for their projects. When they do so, they are not only interested in the technology you developed but also in the support you provide, the frequency of your updates, your product road map, new features and other plans for the future, how you communicate with your users, and how they can become part of your community.

DevRel practitioners, **developer advocates**, and **technical community managers** will come to your documentation for learning materials that they can use in their own communities. They will be on the lookout for best practices they can use and ways to connect with your community.

Documentarians working at companies that use your technology will consult your documentation as they are developing their own content. They might get involved in your community and hopefully contribute to your docs as editors or writers. They will also take note of documentation best practices and use them in their own projects. Your well-crafted documentation will inspire them to develop great documentation sites, and this will raise the bar for others – thus continuously improving the quality of developer documentation available on the Web.

As you can reach so many people in so many different roles, you also have a chance to advocate for causes that are important to you: let your documentation be an example for great performance, accessibility, inclusiveness, sustainability, or any other aspect you deeply care about.

User Interviews

In a user interview, a researcher asks a user questions about a topic with the goal of learning about that topic (e.g., about the use of an application, or the user's habits). User interviews are usually one-on-one sessions.

In the beginning of your discovery process, you focus on *what* the documentation needs to accomplish for your users before getting into *how* it would accomplish it. *What* describes the value your documentation should provide to the user. The *how* is the way in which your docs deliver that value to the user. The *how* is the design, the workflows, and the technology used to implement the documentation. You will focus on the *how* in later phases.

Before conducting user interviews, the UX researcher on your team prepares an interview plan that includes the following:

- Descriptions of the **potential interviewees** that include roles, behaviors, and other relevant attributes. Any (potential) real user is a good candidate for the interview.

- **Goal** of the interview. The interviewer will share this information with the interviewee, and it can also be used to stay on topic during the interview. The goals will be broader in the beginning and get more and more focused as the project progresses.

- **Hypothesis**, a collection of assumptions you want to assess. Did you identify a real problem, a real user need?

- Question pool, a collection of **questions** to ask that you can use to select six to ten questions for the interview.

- **Interview guide**, a description of all the aforementioned aspects and the finalized questions.

We found that semi-structured interviews work very well for this phase. Compared to a structured interview that follows a set of questions that you can't divert from, a semi-structured interview is more open and allows for new ideas to come up during the interview.

A practical example for the initial interviews could be two or three rounds of (online) interviews with eight to ten users of your product or members of your team. The goal of the interviews at this stage could be centered around learning more about your target audience segments, their documentation needs and expectations, and the problems you want to solve with your documentation site.

Once you have the results of these initial interviews, collect them in a report and share them with your team and community to collect their feedback.

When you have collected enough information to move on and define your personas and content needs, you are ready to progress to the Define phase of the Design Thinking process. Remember, the process is nonlinear, so you can – and probably will – come back to the Empathize phase in the future.

Personas

During the discovery phase, you begin to develop an understanding of the types of users that will be interacting with your documentation site. Based on the information you have available, you can create proto-personas or personas to describe their characteristics. **Proto-personas** are based on the assumptions of stakeholders; they represent what you think your users are like. They are typically utilized in the startup product world, especially during the phase of searching for market fit. **Personas** are based on actual research data. You will have to revisit and revalidate both types of personas multiple times during later phases of the process and any time there is a shift in the target audience segments, but proto-personas need a validation early on for you to be able to work with them.

When you hold workshops with your team members to explore and ideate about personas, you will get proto-personas as a result – and more: as you involve your team members, they gradually get to know your users better and become more and more empathetic toward them. When you ask your team members about your users and then validate the results later with real users, many different outcomes are possible. Perhaps you'll find that your team knows your users quite well and your proto-personas only need some minor adjustments, or you might realize that your users are very different from how you imagined them. In all cases, by the time you develop your personas, your team is more engaged with and closer to understanding your users than they would have been without getting involved. Developing proto-personas and later validating them is also the approach you can take if your product has no real users yet.

Each persona has specific goals and behaviors that differentiate them from the others. This helps you identify which features of the site they are likely to use and how. From the technical writer's perspective, they are essential: they give you the illusion of a person you are writing to. Even if they will be reevaluated and changed later, they are necessary to be able to start writing any kind of content. Personas also help team members share a specific, consistent understanding of various audience groups. You can use these personas to see how well proposed solutions meet their needs and to prioritize features based on how well they address the needs of one or more personas.

Persona descriptions can include any relevant information about the persona, but each description should include the same aspects for consistency. For personas of a developer documentation site, we found that describing the following aspects proved to be helpful:

- A fictional **name** and **photo** that makes the persona easier to relate and refer to

- **Role**, job title, major responsibilities

- **Keywords** that quickly help us identify the main characteristics of a persona

- **Goals** that describe what the user would like to accomplish

- **Behavior** that describes what the user does as part of their job or as a learning strategy

- Factors you **must** keep in mind to fulfill the persona's needs (e.g., you have to provide step-by-step guidance for a junior developer to set up their environment)

- What you **must not** do (for example, don't show complex solutions first to a user with entry-level knowledge)

As an example, Figure 2-1 shows early descriptions of the personas of the platformOS Documentation.

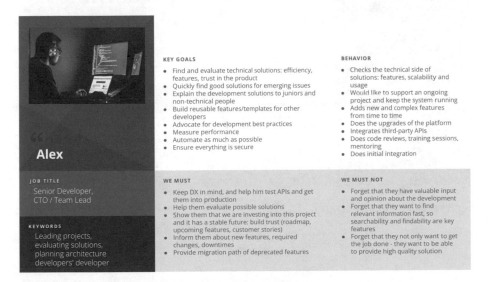

Figure 2-1. *Initial personas of the platformOS Documentation*

KEY GOALS

- Find answers to questions (troubleshooting)
- Have a smooth onboarding process
- Check out example solutions to see how to set up features
- Relies on senior developers in the team to provide guidance

BEHAVIOR

- Has mid-level knowledge without much experience, therefore would like to see examples to figure out how to start
- Searches for solutions to see how others previously solved the same issue
- Follows others' best practices
- Prototype new features with existing code generators
- Reaches out to other members of the team for help
- Fixes bugs

Jennifer

JOB TITLE
Junior Developer

KEYWORDS
Solving tasks, working in a team

WE MUST

- Use clear technical communication
- Help them get started
- Show examples that are easy to reproduce to explain the thinking behind the code
- Help them setup development environment quickly
- Provide explanation of common errors/troubleshooting
- Stress the importance of security
- Stress the importance of performance
- Clearly state cost implications of using a feature

WE MUST NOT

- Think that they can figure out the solution based on their experience
- Forget that they have valuable input about what kind of support would fit their knowledge level
- Assume understanding/realizing of performance implications of a chosen solution

KEY GOALS

- Solve tasks on the marketplaces as well and as quickly as possible
- Find examples that match specific site-building goals to use as inspiration
- Adjust existing marketplaces or templates
- Create reporting tools for administrators

BEHAVIOR

- Has basic or entry-level knowledge without experience, therefore they are uncertain about next steps
- Uses code examples to copy-paste
- Asks for help to find answers to questions
- Gets the job done but quality/reusability/performance are rather irrelevant
- Often works alone, without team support, as a freelancer

Thomas

JOB TITLE
Site Builder

KEYWORDS
Entry-level development knowledge, Freelancer, Small team specialised in platformOS integration

WE MUST

- Use clear technical communication
- Guide them through the processes with easy to understand step-by-step tutorials
- Help them learn how the marketplace works
- Provide a QA page where they can find answers to most common questions

WE MUST NOT

- Forget that although they have limited technical knowledge they can learn along the way and improve
- Show them complex solutions first
- Assume they understand or even read error messages
- Assume they know how to copy/paste examples which they need to modify

Figure 2-1. *(continued)*

KEY GOALS
- Has a marketplace that works well
- Improves the site based on her needs
- Day to day management of the site
- Monitor users of marketplace
- Measure usage of features on the marketplace
- Analytics - users/payments/ROI/other business parameters
- Create a quick POC for a new idea

BEHAVIOR
- Doesn't do developer work but would like to know the status and progress of the marketplace platform
- Tries to find the best features to improve her marketplace
- Plans A/B tests
- Checks the growth of the marketplace

Clara

JOB TITLE
Marketplace Owners, Sales / Marketing, Project Owner

KEYWORDS
Business perspective, Security, Trustworthiness, Reliable / Stable

WE MUST
- Add non-technical descriptions about the marketplace
- Share customer stories with her
- Explain why our product is a good fit, share a list of features

WE MUST NOT
- Use technical communication with her

We will focus on and develop this persona in a later phase.

Figure 2-1. *(continued)*

Content Inventory

Once you are done with the initial discovery and have defined the personas for your documentation, you can proceed to creating a content inventory. As per its definition, a content inventory is a list of all of the content you have – but in this case, you will add all the content you don't have yet but know you will need, too.

Collect and evaluate all existing content first.

If you already have a documentation site, you can add data about each topic to a spreadsheet like topic title, URL, last updated, author(s), target audience, navigation level, topic type, or others. You can use a website crawler (like Screaming Frog's SEO Spider[9] or SEMRush[10]) to extract data for your inventory.

---

[9]https://www.screamingfrog.co.uk/seo-spider/
[10]https://www.semrush.com/

Even if you don't have a documentation site yet, you might have some notes, readmes, blog posts, or diagrams that you will be able to use. You might have had some demos or webinars about the product that you can also use to gather information from. Think about what you can reuse from these assets and how much work it would be to adjust them.

Based on the needs of your personas and the competitor research, you can add all the content that you don't have yet but think you'll need.

A developer documentation site typically needs content like the following:

- Onboarding tutorials and concept topics (different personas usually need different onboarding journeys)

- Concept topics and tutorials for different features of the product (for different experience levels)

- Use cases, best practices (for experienced developers, but useful for all skill levels and other target audience segments as well)

- References (like API reference, error messages)

- Road map

- Try-out section, sandbox

- Information for contributors

- Information for community involvement

- Ways to get involved in user research

- Results of past user research activities

- Ways to provide feedback

- Ways to get support

- Legal information (copyright, license, privacy policy)

The content can include text, code snippets, images, or videos.

Figure 2-2 shows the first content inventory of the platformOS Documentation prepared for a card sorting exercise.

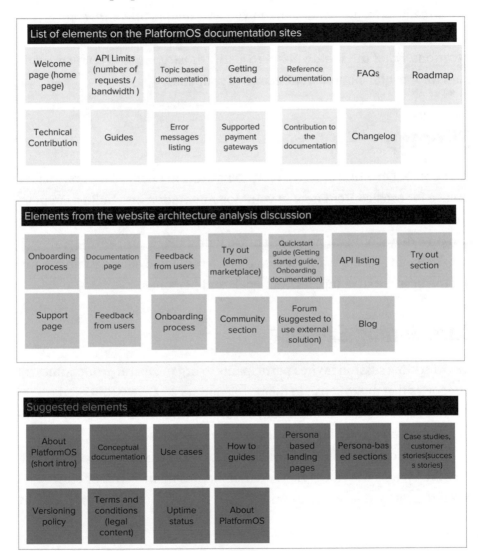

Figure 2-2. *The first content inventory of the platformOS Documentation*

You are familiar with the documentation sites of your competitors and understand the challenges, pain points, and expectations of your users. You have a clear definition of who your users are *(personas)*, what content you already have, and what content you will need *(content inventory)*. You now probably have some ideas for the main goals of the first couple iterations. Enter the **Ideate** phase to clarify those goals and come up with a plan for the information architecture of your site.

Sitemap

Your content inventory is a list of content without much structure. To find a place for each content item in your documentation and build a sitemap, you have to find a way to learn how your users think about your content and how they would interact with it. We found that a card sorting exercise is an efficient and enjoyable way to define connected elements and map out the best site structure for your goals and personas.

Card Sorting Exercise

A card sorting session invites participants to organize and group topics into categories that make sense to them. To conduct a card sorting exercise, you can use cards or post-its in person, or card sorting or whiteboard software solutions like Miro[11], Mural[12], or FigJam[13] for online sessions.

Card sorting exercises are considered open when the participants have to come up with the categories and their names themselves, or closed when the categories are predefined. Here, you will work with the topics in

---

[11]https://miro.com/

[12]https://www.mural.co/

[13]https://www.figma.com/figjam/

your content inventory, so it's beneficial to keep the card sorting exercise open to learn what categories your users would find meaningful on your site and how they would label them.

Figure 2-3 shows a screen from Mural during the initial card sorting workshop of the platformOS Documentation. As the first exercise, we introduced the personas and then asked the participants to share their thoughts on them. Participants decided if they agree or disagree with the statements listed under the personas, and they could add what they thought was missing. In the end, we discussed everything and tried to come up with a group consensus. Once we arrived at the consensus, we considered the personas validated (for now).

Figure 2-3. *Screen showing the persona validation process*

Figure 2-4 shows another screen from the card sorting session. The task was to group connected elements to visualize the relations between the different items. This helped us to define the larger areas of the site and how elements relate to them.

Cards on the board were color-coded:

- Yellow cards are existing content elements.

- Green cards contain elements from the stakeholder interviews during the Empathize phase.

- Orange cards are suggested elements that we collected based on the articulated problems and needs.

- The four shades of pink represent the four personas.

Figure 2-4. *Screen from the initial card sorting session showing connected elements grouped together*

Cards grouped together belong together, so they should be displayed in the same section or under the same menu item on your documentation site. Based on the content inventory and the results of the card sorting sessions, you can outline a sitemap for your future site. The sitemap shows the structure of your site.

Figure 2-5 shows the first sitemap of the platformOS Documentation that we created based on the results of the card sorting session. If you check out our documentation, you will find that through years of iterative changes and improvements, a lot of it has changed by now.

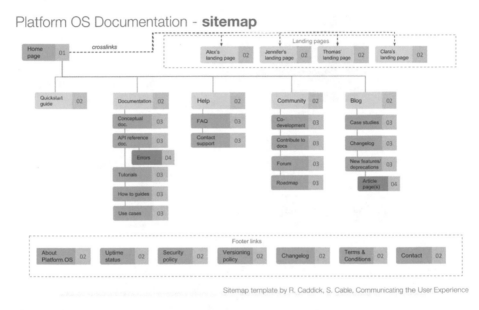

Platform OS Documentation - **sitemap**

Sitemap template by R. Caddick, S. Cable, Communicating the User Experience

Figure 2-5. *The first sitemap of the platformOS Documentation*

You can also use your sitemap as a part of your road map to keep track of site improvements, content needs, and project phases. As you follow an iterative process, it's helpful to create several sitemaps – one for each iteration.

Figure 2-6 shows sitemaps of the platformOS Documentation created for the first and second iterations.

platformOS Developers **sitemap - round 1**

platformOS Developers **sitemap - round 2**

Figure 2-6. *Sitemaps created for different iterations*

Persona-Based Content Prioritization

When you put the information you have about your personas and your sitemap into context, you can outline coherent stories. These stories are similar to user journeys and show the order of actions the user personas take while interacting with the site. During the card sorting sessions, you explore areas of interest for each user persona which shows you where to focus first. You can also validate the importance of each area to assign higher priorities to the ones that are more important for your users.

Figure 2-7 shows how we highlighted the areas of interest for one of the personas (Thomas) during the card sorting sessions. Thomas' cards were the dark pink ones, so we could clearly visualize the areas this persona is primarily interested in. We did this for all personas.

Figure 2-7. *Highlighted areas of interest based on the persona's actions taken on the site*

You can now display each persona's interactions with the site on the sitemap. Figure 2-8 shows the first version of the platformOS Documentation sitemap with the Site Builder persona's journeys added.

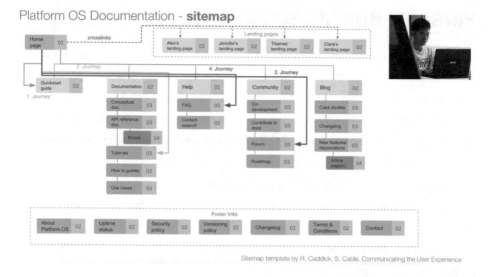

Figure 2-8. *Persona interactions with the site displayed on the sitemap*

Note   You probably noticed that the spelling of our company name, platformOS, is not consistent on these screenshots. That's because we started developing our documentation very early on, even before the brand was finalized.

Workshops for creating and validating personas, a content inventory, or a sitemap provides an opportunity for your team members to collaborate and get engaged with the documentation project early on. Each time you discuss different opinions, include different points of view, validate your assumptions, and learn more about your users, the foundations for your documentation become stronger.

Summary

This chapter demonstrated the important role user research plays in the discovery phase of building a developer documentation site. It introduced user research practices and processes that help you learn more about your users, their goals, behaviors, and documentation needs. To conduct all the research you need and analyze the results, a UX researcher will be an invaluable member of your documentation team.

You got ideas for how to

- Research your **competitors** for insights and ideas

- Conduct **user research** to learn about your target audience, their documentation needs, and the problems you want to solve

- Define **personas**

- Create a **content inventory**

- Create a **sitemap**

- **Prioritize content needs** based on what's most important for your personas

You can now start thinking about your content – but there are still some steps to take before you can actually start writing the docs. First, you have to come up with processes that facilitate content production, contribution, and continuous updates: you'll need an editorial workflow.

CHAPTER 3

Editorial Workflow

The editorial workflow encompasses how you create, edit, publish, and manage content. It is the foundation for the editorial experience you provide, including how you document the processes you developed and how you share it with your contributors.

A great editorial experience will make it easy – even enjoyable – for your team members and external contributors to add or improve documentation content, which means that they will be more willing and more engaged to contribute.

Considering the requirements for a developer documentation site, your editorial workflow should allow all contributors (internal and external) to

- Update existing content and publish new content quickly

- Update content as frequently as needed

- Make small changes (like fixing a typo) or large changes (like adding a new section with many topics at the same time)

- Work on content in parallel

- Rename and update anything in the documentation (e.g., when the name of a software component or feature that is used in multiple places all throughout the documentation changes)

© Diana Lakatos 2023
D. Lakatos, *Crafting Docs for Success*, Design Thinking,
https://doi.org/10.1007/978-1-4842-9594-6_3

- Restructure, reorder, and move topics, and update related navigation and URLs

- Check what changes other contributors have made

- Review and give feedback on changes made by others

- Feel ownership of their contributions

While fulfilling all these requirements, your editorial workflow should correspond to the needs of different contributors. If you choose to follow a Docs-as-Code approach that accommodates your main contributors, developers, you have to think about ways you can adjust your workflow to also cater to other, less-technical contributors. It should also let contributors use any major operating system or tool of their choice. For example, you can define the required format for a topic, but you should let writers and editors use any software application they are comfortable with for writing and editing.

Note   Find out more about helping users with different skill levels contribute to documentation in Chapter 6, "Community."

Finally, your editorial workflow should provide practical processes for making your work easier, like the option to revert changes, keep track of revisions, run tests, or automate processes.

On top of these requirements, you can find ways to include more processes in your editorial workflow. We found that it made sense for us to have all development-related processes in the same workflow from the beginning, and later we extended our editorial workflow with project management–related processes like issue tracking for closer collaboration with our community and more transparency.

Following an iterative process like Design Thinking ensures that you don't have to define and build your whole workflow before the first contributor touches your content. You will test, adjust, and iterate to improve your editorial workflow the same way you work with other parts of your documentation.

Editorial Workflow Example

Let's take an example to understand each step of an editorial workflow. In this case, the workflow is shown from the viewpoint of a community member, as our team includes additional steps like opening an issue, having discussions, and finally closing the issue.

Figure 3-1 shows the steps of the editorial workflow in order:

1. **Write** new content using templates provided by the technical communication team or update existing content.

2. **Submit** the new topic or changes as a pull request to notify reviewers.

3. **Review** changes using a technical and editorial peer-review system.

4. Discuss and **edit** as needed. Repeat steps 3–4 until the change is approved.

5. **Merge** the approved pull request.

6. **Deploy** the changes automatically to staging, then to production if all tests succeeded to publish the new or updated content.

Figure 3-1. *The steps of the editorial workflow example*

We follow the **Docs-as-Code** approach. The platformOS
Documentation is in a separate repository on GitHub, which stores the
code base and the content of our documentation site. Our documentation
is open source, and we found that having it in a separate repository
worked very well with reviewers and contributors. It's also a good setup
for frequent iterations. We have a main branch, and we work locally in a
dedicated branch, and then we send pull requests for review to be merged
into the main branch. Any platformOS user can clone and reuse our
documentation if they would like to use it as a starting point for their docs.

Although our documentation is in a separate repository from the code
of the core product, we use a similar workflow as code repos, including the
use of continuous integration and continuous delivery for publishing. To
preview docs, we use our own staging site, which is an exact copy of the
live documentation site. We release updates frequently: there are times
when we merge multiple changes a day, and there are times when we
merge changes once or twice a week.

Step 1: Writing Content

The process starts with a writing task, for example, when

- We need to fix a typo or other mistakes

- We need to update something because there was a change

- We would like to add a new topic because a new feature was added to our product

- We get internal or external feedback through Slack, the feedback block on our documentation site, user research, team members, engineering, or through any other communication channel

All of these requests are considered tasks, regardless of where they came from. We create a ticket for the task and add it to the backlog of our internal sprint planning, where we discuss priorities and the available capacity. The selected tickets are added for the next sprint.

Then, the author writes new content or makes changes to existing content. The author can be any of our team members, but also any community member; the process is the same for everyone (except, of course, community members don't have to schedule their work according to our sprints). Authors work in their own environments and text editors and follow formatting requirements specified in our documentation style guide. They are encouraged to use pre-made templates for writing different content types. Figure 3-2 shows an author's work in a text editor (Visual Studio Code).

Figure 3-2. *An author working in a text editor*

Step 2: Submitting Content

When the update or new content is done, the author sends a pull request to the documentation GitHub repository.

You don't have to enforce strict rules for commits and PRs but strive to make your commit messages clear and concise. The subject should usually include information about what the commit does (add, fix, etc.) and indicate what part of the documentation was changed. The body includes further information if needed and a preview link where the change can be reviewed on a staging site.

If you want to use your commit history to automatically generate release notes (e.g., using release-please[1] or auto-changelog[2]), you have to make sure that your commit messages have a consistent format. The

---

[1]https://github.com/googleapis/release-please
[2]https://github.com/cookpete/auto-changelog

Conventional Commits[3] specification provides a lightweight set of rules for creating a commit message history you can build automation on.

In a pull request that is related to an issue, we use GitHub's reference feature. We add the issue number in PRs prefaced with "Fixes", "Closes", or "Resolves". For example, "Fixes #1638". This way, when the PR is merged into the main branch, it also automatically closes the issue.

Step 3: Review

The review process starts with the open PR. Reviewers can be assigned, or team members responsible for our documentation can also take on review tasks themselves. We review the content and add comments or suggestions, and we can also discuss specific changes right on the PR.

A writer and a subject matter expert review all changes.

Writers check for language and grammar, formatting, ease of comprehension, and style guide compliance. Small edits, like grammar or formatting fixes, can be made by a writer without the need for further review. Subject matter experts like developers or UX researchers verify that the information in the pull request is accurate. Developers also test example code before it's approved.

We regularly test for accessibility with various tools and ensure that the site complies with all accessibility requirements. We also check for accessible and inclusive language as specified in our style guide.

The developer experience that your documentation provides goes way beyond the features and content on your documentation site. How contribution works, how you communicate with your team members and users, and how inclusive your community is all play important parts in your DX. Reviews are one of the ways you can collaborate and communicate with your users, so you should be mindful of the **review culture** you foster.

---

[3]https://www.conventionalcommits.org/

Step 4: Editing

In the editing phase, contributors and reviewers work together to improve the submitted update. Suggestions can be discussed in a message thread and committed to the branch of the update. Discussions on the PR often improve the update by raising the need for more context and clarification that are then added to the content.

Step 5: Merging Changes

The review and editing phase closes when all contributors and reviewers agree, all edits have been committed, and the PR is approved by all reviewers. Once the PR is final, we merge it. Figure 3-3 shows an example where two reviewers have approved the (now merged) PR.

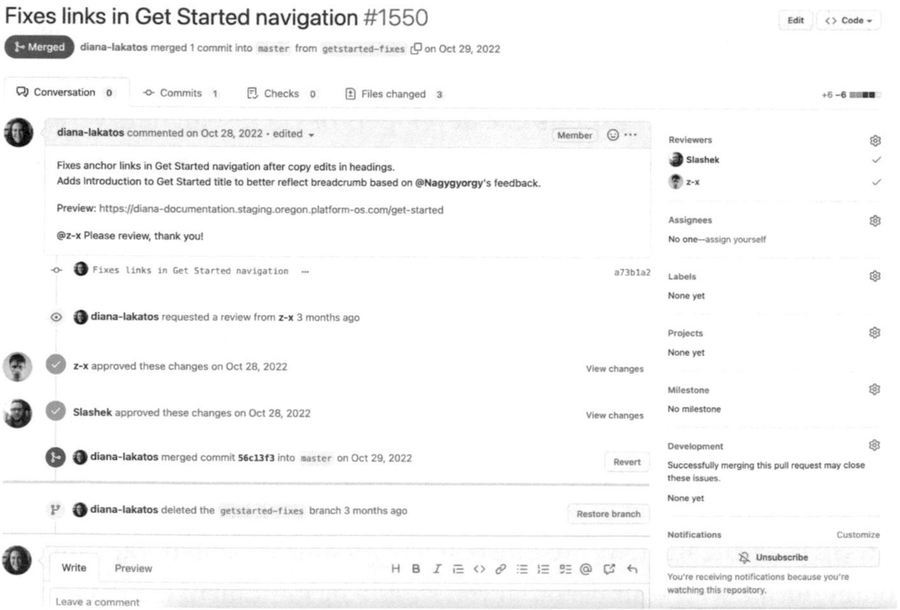

Figure 3-3. *Approvals of two reviewers on a merged PR*

Step 6: Deployment

We employ continuous integration and continuous delivery using GitHub Actions. New content undergoes automated testing, and if all tests pass successfully, it is deployed first to our staging site and then to our production site. Figure 3-4 displays deployed changes on the GitHub Actions interface.

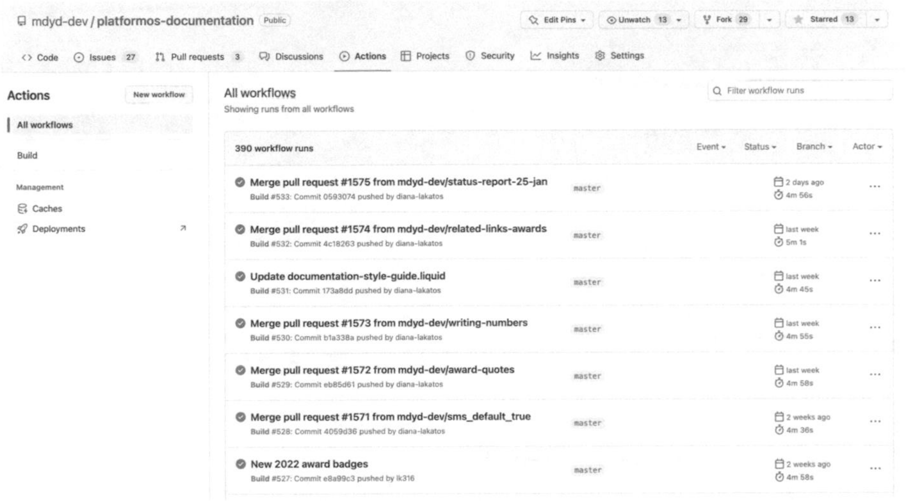

Figure 3-4. *Deployed changes on the GitHub Actions interface*

The whole process from ticket creation to merging the PR is fully transparent, and anyone can see and contribute to it at any step on GitHub.

We documented and shared our editorial workflow in our Contributor Guide and in the README of our GitHub repository.

Issue Management

Besides handling the whole editorial workflow on GitHub, we decided to extend the use of this tool to project management tasks, too. We keep track of content needs and content production on the Issues[4] interface of our documentation repository. Anyone can open an issue, and it can be any

---

[4]https://github.com/features/issues

type of task, a bug that needs fixing, a topic request, or some feedback on existing topics or plans that we have shared. Figure 3-5 shows a list of open issues for the platformOS Documentation.

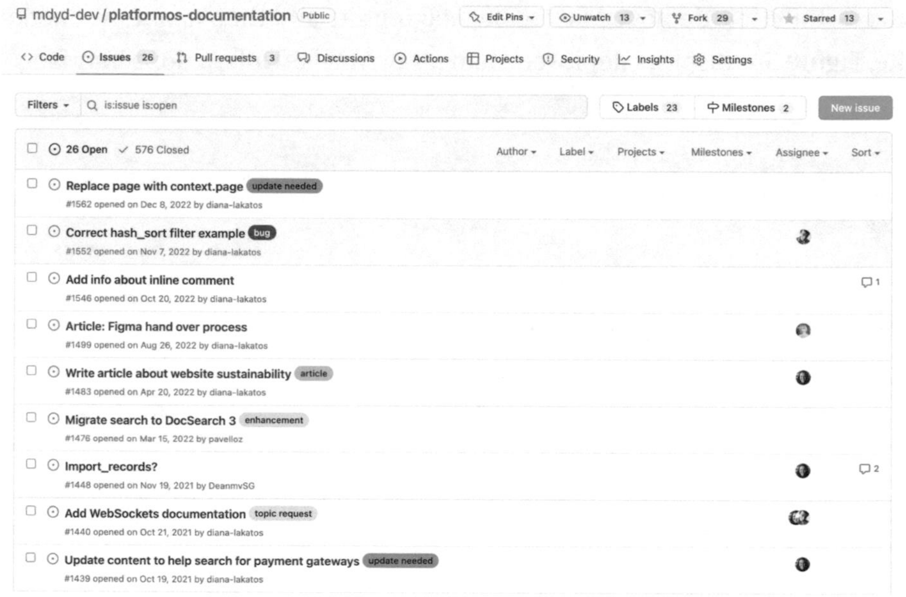

Figure 3-5. *Issues on the GitHub Issues interface*

Tickets or issues should include all necessary information for everyone involved to be able to understand the task:

- **Issue title:** A clear and concise summary of the task. It is useful to start the title with a verb that refers to the type of the task (write, edit, update, fix, etc.) and include what the task refers to (which topic, navigation, etc.).

- **Description:** A sufficient description of the task and the desired result. The PR with the update refers to the issue, so it should be specific enough for reviewers to be able to determine whether the change solves the issue. If the issue is related to an existing documentation topic, add the link to the topic in the issue. Bug descriptions should include steps to reproduce the problem and screenshots if applicable.

- **References:** Issues can refer to other related issues. This shows cross-connected issues that you can navigate between. GitHub provides a drop-down list to select issues for cross-linking.

- **Mentions:** We use mentions to reference our team or community members. Mentions typically use an "@" symbol followed by the member's username. This way, the mentioned person gets notifications about the issue and any further changes on the issue.

- **Labels:** Labels provide categories that you define ahead of time. We use labels to indicate the type of a task like *topic request, bug,* or *update needed.* We also use them to indicate if they are for the core product or for modules, to assign priorities, or to mark if an issue is blocked. An issue can have multiple labels that you can use for filtering.

- **Milestones:** GitHub Milestones allow you to group together multiple issues or pull requests into a cohesive group, which represents a specific project, feature, or time period. We sometimes use milestones when we have a large task that can be broken down into smaller issues, for example, when we do our accessibility review and edits. Milestones can also be used for organizing issues related to different iterations.

- **Projects:** We have two projects defined for our documentation site in the issue tracker; one of them is for issues that are related to content like writing topics and updating existing topics, and the other one is for development tasks on the documentation site, for example, if something needs to be fixed on the front end.

- **Assignees:** We assign people to tasks to know who is responsible for managing or accomplishing that task.

Figure 3-6 shows an example of a (now closed) issue.

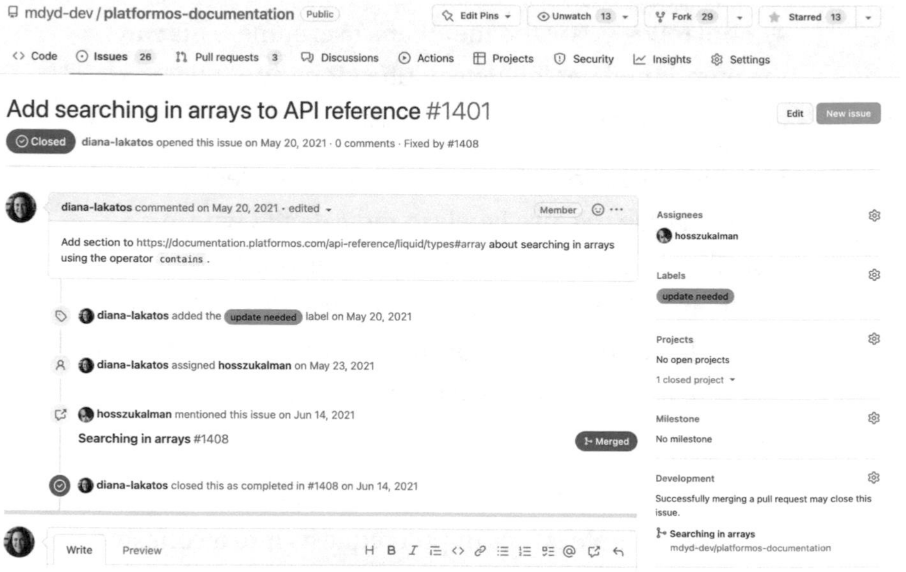

Figure 3-6. *A closed issue on the GitHub Issues interface*

You want your issues, commits, and PRs organized and your processes well defined, but you don't want to overwhelm your team and community with unnecessary administration. Experiment with different rules and formats to find the right balance for your contributors. For example, as a lightweight process, ensure that your team consistently includes clear issue titles and detailed descriptions (with a preview link when applicable), assigns reviewers and team members, and sets labels. As the next steps, consider introducing issue templates, particularly if you are also experimenting with automation for creating release notes and changelogs that require a specific issue title format. Additionally, plan regular reviews for issues, prioritize them based on their impact and urgency, and make sure to document the entire process to facilitate onboarding for new team members and community contributors.

When discussing issues, make sure to either discuss them in the issue comments or write a summary on the issue if the discussion happened in real life, over video conferencing, or in chat. You can refer back to this information later, and all your team members and (if your issue tracking is public) community members have access to the same information and can get involved if they would like to participate in the conversation.

Review Culture

Reviews are a great opportunity to communicate with your users (both inside and outside of your organization), transfer knowledge, enjoy collaboration, and, ultimately, improve your documentation. Although they are part of the day-to-day work of people in various roles, like technical writers, developers, and other SMEs, reviews rarely get the attention that other communication channels do. In the case of open source documentation, where communication during reviews is public, not only do they tell your users about your team culture, they contribute to the overall community culture as well.

There are many ways to ensure that you create and maintain an inclusive review culture.

As an author, work on your draft (and mark it as a work in progress) until it's ready to be reviewed. You can of course ask the opinions of others and brainstorm about improving your writing before you submit it for review, but by the time you request a review, the PR should be reasonably complete. This doesn't mean it has to be perfect at all, but it helps if you fully described what you wanted to convey and you tried to follow the style guide and any applicable templates.

Be respectful of reviewers' time. Provide context in the PR or related issue so that reviewers have all the background information they need to start reviewing your content.

It also helps to scope your PR well. Topic-based authoring precisely defines the units of information when you are contributing whole topics, and in the case of larger updates spanning more topics, it's worth thinking about how you could break down the task into smaller but logical chunks. The PR should be complete in the sense that if it is approved and merged, no information is missing, and it does not disrupt the documentation until another PR is merged.

As a reviewer, you can lean on the grammar of the language used, the style guide, and templates to objectively review documentation content. The style guide should specify the tone and style the company uses. If you have an improvement suggestion, discuss it with the author. Make sure that while you focus on what to improve, you notice what the author has done well and give out compliments. The review is an important part of the editorial workflow, and your team should treat it as such. Reserve your capacity for doing the review without any interruptions or time pressure.

Subject matter experts reviewing documentation should ensure that the information is accurate and complete, and developers should confirm that code examples work as intended and that the steps described in processes lead to the outcomes specified.

Based on our experience, new reviewers greatly benefit from having clear expectations, which your Documentation Style Guide can effectively assist with, and from being paired with an experienced reviewer at the beginning. Experimenting with a review checklist might also be a good idea.

Open reviews foster a collaborative environment, providing an opportunity for people to get involved and contribute a variety of perspectives and expertise, which can potentially uncover gaps or ambiguities.

As authors and reviewers communicate, always seek to understand. Ask open questions to clarify intentions, and be receptive to new perspectives. Know that everyone regardless of their skill level can contribute meaningfully. Strive to communicate with compassion, kindness, and awareness of yourself and others.

Summary

This chapter delved into the topic of creating an editorial workflow for your developer documentation site that discussed

- What an editorial workflow is and how it benefits your documentation

- The steps of an editorial workflow through a real-life example and what happens at each step

- How you can extend your editorial workflow with issue management

- Why fostering an inclusive review culture is important

Now that you have your editorial workflow planned and set up, you can start thinking about producing content: choosing a format, writing a style guide, and creating templates.

CHAPTER 4

Content Production

Following the Content First approach means that you start developing content (or at least defining the structure of your content) relatively early on in your process before you start working on wireframes, layouts, or the technical implementation.

When building the foundations for your developer documentation, you created a **content inventory** that showed what content you already have and what content you will need. Now, to be able to produce that content, you should come up with a system that ensures that the quality of the content you produce will be good and content all over your documentation will be consistent. You are still following an iterative approach, so don't worry about getting it perfect the first time around but the better system you develop, the easier it will be to create content for your documentation, maintain or improve its quality, and involve internal and external contributors.

Note   Documentation quality is discussed in more detail in Chapter 10, "Measures of Success."

To start content production, you'll have to

- Think about what markup language you will use

- Start writing your documentation style guide

- Create templates for the most used content types

© Diana Lakatos 2023
D. Lakatos, *Crafting Docs for Success*, Design Thinking,
https://doi.org/10.1007/978-1-4842-9594-6_4

Markup Languages

Markup languages are text-encoding systems that control the structure and formatting of the text by a set of symbols inserted into the text. They are used for rendered documents, meaning that you write content in your own text editor and publish it through a process that turns the text and markup into a formatted document.

If you can choose the tools you work with freely, you can approach the selection of the markup language from the perspective of your contributors (writers, reviewers, editors).

Docs-as-Code workflows usually use a **lightweight markup syntax** that allows authors to create formatted text that is then displayed in a web browser. They aim to be easy to use and are not connected to any standards organizations. Many Docs-as-Code workflows use the lightweight markup syntax **Markdown**.

Markdown was created by John Gruber with the goal of simplifying HTML, and while others adopted and adjusted it to best fit their needs, slightly different versions of the standard called "flavors" were created like GitHub Flavored Markdown[1], Leanpub Flavoured Markdown[2], or CommonMark[3]. CommonMark is a standardized specification of the Markdown syntax, aiming to provide a more consistent and unambiguous definition of Markdown compared to the various versions that exist.

The Markdown syntax is straightforward. It uses symbols to achieve what HTML tags do; for example, to format a bulleted list, you use * or - instead of the ul tag.

Figure 4-1 shows the Markdown syntax on the left and its preview on the right in the Visual Studio Code editor.

---

[1]https://github.github.com/gfm/
[2]https://leanpub.com/lfm/read
[3]https://commonmark.org/

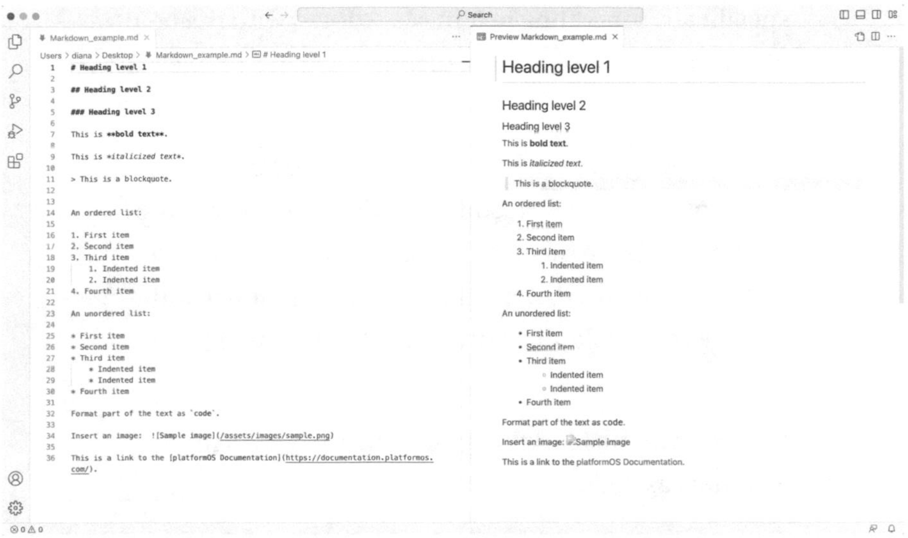

Figure 4-1. *Example Markdown syntax*

Markdown is a great fit for developer documentation because of the following:

- The tools you use in a Docs-as-Code workflow often use the Markdown syntax. GitHub automatically renders Markdown files with the md extension into HTML. Many static site generators used to publish documentation also use Markdown.

- Markdown is a versatile markup that provides semantic meaning for content while still being quite easy to read, which is especially helpful for reviewers.

- Contributors can use their editor of choice to write and edit documentation content. Most text or code editors like VS Code or Sublime Text have built-in or downloadable extensions for Markdown syntax highlighting and preview functions. Markdown editors specifically for editing text in Markdown with the help of a formatting toolbar and displaying a live preview are also available.

- Most developers, writers, and editors are familiar with Markdown, and even if someone doesn't know it, they can usually learn the basics fast, or use a Markdown editor. Templates that are already in Markdown and include the whole structure make the learning process even easier.

- You can run the Markdown files through the same workflow as code.

- The OpenAPI specification allows the use of the CommonMark version of Markdown for rich text representation in `description` fields. This means that Markdown can be a good choice for API documentation.

- Semantic HTML is crucial for accessibility. By ensuring you style text using a markup language that translates into HTML, you enable screen readers to navigate the content effectively. For example, it's important to know how to add alt text to images in Markdown. Since navigation pointers rely on heading levels, ensure you're correctly indicating headings using Markdown syntax, rather than resorting to bold text to create headings.

Figure 4-2 shows a page from the platformOS Documentation written in Markdown. Our documentation site uses Liquid pages, but we write documentation content in Markdown and use a Markdown converter to turn it into Liquid.

Figure 4-2. A documentation page written in Markdown

There are some drawbacks to working with Markdown that you will have to be aware of. As the goal with Markdown is to keep the syntax simple, not all HTML elements have a corresponding Markdown tag. If you want to use formatting not covered by Markdown, you can directly insert HTML tags into your Markdown file.

As I mentioned, Markdown is not regulated and maintained by a standards committee, so the different versions or flavors are inconsistent. Always check what version of Markdown the tool you would like to use (e.g., a static site generator) supports. To prevent confusion, always specify the Markdown version you use and link to its specification in your documentation style guide.

Migrating content written in Markdown to a different flavor might work when you only use elements that are common among the two flavors, but migrating to other markup languages can become a more complex task. Markdown used to be incompatible with DITA, but the Lightweight DITA specification aims to define mappings between XML, HTML5, and Markdown that would enable authoring, collaboration, and publishing across different markup languages.

It's also worth noting some advancements in the realm of Markdown, specifically the MDX[4] format and tools like Docusaurus[5]. MDX combines Markdown's simplicity with JSX's (a syntax extension to JavaScript) interactive capabilities, allowing the use of React components within Markdown files for advanced features. Docusaurus is an open source tool for creating documentation websites that integrates with MDX, offering dynamic content within Markdown files.

AsciiDoc[6] and **reStructuredText**[7] are two markup languages besides Markdown that are often discussed in relation to documentation. They both provide more semantic richness and are based on standards, so they can be used more consistently. GitHub supports both, and you can find many static site generators that support them, like Asciidoctor or Sphinx.

These markup languages are solid choices for building a documentation site, but keeping in mind how much your documentation can benefit from internal and external developer contributors, making contributing as easy as possible for them makes Markdown the most obvious choice for developer documentation in my experience.

Documentation Style Guide

When you start thinking about the content you'll create, you inevitably start contemplating different aspects like tone, style, formatting, and others. You'll make your job (and the job of your contributors and

---

[4]https://mdxjs.com/
[5]https://docusaurus.io/
[6]https://asciidoc.org/
[7]https://docutils.sourceforge.io/rst.html

reviewers) that much easier if you write down all of these decisions as you arrive at them. The collection of these decisions will become your documentation style guide: guidelines for making your writing grammatically correct, clear, concise, and consistent, while always addressing the specific needs of your target audience segments. It will also include guidelines for using images and videos, so it will be the main rulebook contributors, reviewers (including accessibility reviewers), and editors can use.

If this seems like a hefty task, you might be happy to know that you've already started working on it during the discovery phase: you researched the audience who will use your documentation and defined your personas in detail. You also thought about different topic types and the markup language you'd like to use. Developing your documentation style guide is an iterative process, where you add your guidelines and improve them by using and testing them, and asking for feedback as your contributors write, review, and edit content on your documentation.

This section provides explanations for the different sections of a minimum viable developer documentation style guide and a checklist that you can use as a starting point and to track your progress. You don't have to include everything right away. You can be confident that if you always add guidelines as the questions and decisions come up during content production, you'll soon have a usable style guide that covers most of what your contributors need.

Introduction

In the introduction of your style guide, address your audience, thank your contributors, describe the goal of the style guide, and set expectations by sharing what topics are explained.

Audience

Anyone who contributes to your documentation will need to understand who they are writing for, so describe your target audience segments in as much detail as needed. You can test and validate if the level of detail corresponds to the needs of your contributors. Here, you can reuse all the information you collected about the personas in the discovery phase, and if you prepared graphics or diagrams about your personas, you can experiment with including those as well. We found that it's helpful to also add a short definition of what a persona is and how personas are used.

Writing Guidelines

Specify the **language and spelling** you use. If you use English, specify if contributors should follow the rules of British or American English.

We found that it's practical to refer to an existing style guide that covers rules and instructions for using correct grammar and spelling and only highlight the most important rules you want contributors to follow, where your editor team finds contributors often make mistakes, or rules specific to your brand, like your brand voice. Make sure to select a style guide that is available online.

Some classic style guides originally intended for print publications can also be used as the foundations for writing documentation content, for example, the Associated Press Stylebook (AP Stylebook[8]) or the Chicago Manual of Style[9].

You can also refer to or get inspiration from style guides of enterprise software companies, especially those that also have a developer audience,

---

[8]https://www.apstylebook.com/
[9]https://www.chicagomanualofstyle.org/home.html

like the Apple Style Guide[10], Microsoft Writing Style Guide[11], Google Developer Documentation Style Guide[12], or Red Hat Technical Writing Style Guide[13].

It's helpful to include the correct spelling of your product and technologies you mention often for consistency.

When you describe the **tone** of your documentation, you can get inspiration from the voice of your brand, but overall, documentation style guides usually define a clear, simple, friendly, and conversational tone.

Based on our experience, it's helpful to highlight that contributors should use **present tense** in general and avoid using future tense where possible. We also remind them to talk to the users in the **second person**, address the user as "you," and avoid the use of gender-specific, third-person pronouns such as he, she, his, and hers and the use of we, except when we want to emphasize something that the platformOS team did. One exception to these rules we added is to use the first-person singular pronoun "I" in the question part of FAQs.

During reviews and editing, we found that many contributors tend to use passive voice more often than necessary, so we added the rule to write in **active voice**. Active-voice sentences are more direct and easier to understand than passive-voice sentences, so they are a better fit for technical content. This doesn't mean that you should never use passive voice but you should be conscious of your choice and prefer the use of active voice in most cases.

For consistency all throughout your documentation, add rules for the **capitalization** of titles, headings, and terms specific to your product. It's helpful to explain what the title case and sentence case are. Explain basic rules for **punctuation**, for example, in titles and list items, and take a stand

---

[10]https://support.apple.com/en-gb/guide/applestyleguide/welcome/web
[11]https://learn.microsoft.com/en-us/style-guide/welcome/
[12]https://developers.google.com/style
[13]https://stylepedia.net/

on whether you want your contributors to use the **serial comma** or not and stick to the approach you chose. Clarify how you want contributors to write **numbers** – when to use numerals and when to spell out numbers.

Add guidelines for using **lists**. Explain to use numbered lists for sequential task steps and bullet lists for sets of options, notes, and the like. We found it was helpful to specify the format for lists, such as preceding an ordered or bulleted list with a sentence or phrase ending in a colon, beginning each item with a capital letter, how to use periods at the end of list items, and making list items "parallel," for example, starting each item with a verb in the same tense and form.

Add **examples** to all rules to show and compare the desired style and what to avoid. All of these guidelines will help contributors, reviewers, and editors produce clear, concise, and consistent content.

Format

Your contributors need clear guidance on the format they should use, so specify the markup language you use and link to resources like a reference or cheat sheet. If you use Markdown, you might want to explain that there are different versions and clarify which version you use.

Although we link to a Markdown reference in our documentation style guide, we also found it useful to explain how to format the most often used elements, like headings, code samples, or tables. You can also recommend applications that provide a WYSIWYG experience for editing text in the required format, or helpful tools like an online table generator.

Images

Specify the image formats and dimensions you use on your documentation site, and explain when to use which, for example, that JPEG format is best for photos (images with a lot of colors), while PNGs are best for less diverse images. Explain when to use and when not to use images; for example, use images to visualize a process or concept, or show the result of browser rendering if helpful, but don't use images to show code, or an example server response; use code formatting instead.

Potential additional specifications for images could include

- Internationalization or localization, along with translation guidelines

- Guidelines on whether image annotations, such as legends pointing out different screen areas, are allowed or encouraged

- Rules on whether captions are mandatory

- Accessibility requirements, such as contrast, color choice, and alt text

- Information on whether your output automatically adds numbers to image and figure captions

- Details on whether your output enables zoom-in on images with a click

Explain how to insert images with an example.

Videos

Explain how contributors can insert videos, for example, if they have to use a streaming service to upload the video first, and if so, how to use the embed code. You might consider informing them about a time limit for the video length, or specifying screen size and resolution requirements. If you have tips for them to use for recording videos or screencasts, include those as well.

Note   When we started content production, we focused on written content. We found this was a good way to think about and establish the content structure without distractions, and it fit our iterative process well. For quite a while, we changed large chunks of our content frequently, so it helped that we didn't have to modify images or re-record videos whenever something changed. Today still, we are very intentional about adding images and videos.

Accessibility and Inclusive Language

You should continuously work on making your documentation more accessible and usable to the widest possible audience. One ingredient to achieving this goal is writing accessible and inclusive content. Collecting guidelines for accessibility in your documentation style guide brings this aspect to the attention of your contributors, reviewers, and editors.

Note   I explore best practices for writing accessible and inclusive documentation content in more detail in Chapter 7, "Accessibility and Inclusion."

Templates

Even many writers feel uncomfortable in front of a blank page, so it's easy to imagine how a contributor would feel if they had to write a new topic from scratch. Providing some guidance, an outline, or a structure they can start from removes this obstacle. A template is such an outline that includes all nonchangeable content and placeholders with explanations for the parts to add. Placeholders provide information on the recommended format (e.g., title) and any requirements or limitations (e.g., maximum number of characters). Contributors can copy a template and edit it in their own editor. As templates are written in the markup language of your choice, they also help contributors who are not yet familiar with the markup.

Templates also ensure that your documentation stays consistent, and each topic type has the same structure. They help contributors think about the information they need to include and can help enforce topic-based authoring by providing the framework for what a topic is and how to connect related topics.

When we started outlining the structure for our documentation, we started with three main content types inspired by DITA: tutorials that describe how to accomplish a **task**, **concepts** that provide background information and context, and **references** like our API reference. As we added more content, we developed templates for other types of content, like release notes and use cases as well.

Note   The templates I share here are excerpts from the open source platformOS Documentation Style Guide licensed under the terms of the Creative Commons Attribution 4.0 International License. Feel free to reuse content from these templates, adjust them as you see fit, or use them as inspiration.

Concept Topic Template

Concept topics provide essential information that the user needs to know to understand a system, product, or solution. Contributors should write a concept topic to introduce a new feature, describe an idea, or explain how a process works.

The concept topic always includes the following:

- **Title:** A concise description of what the topic is about. We prefer to use nouns in concept topic titles to differentiate them from tutorials right at the title level, for example, Pages.

- **Definition:** A clear definition of the concept topic that answers the question "what." Based on the previous example for the title, the definition would explain what pages are, why they are used, and what their benefits are.

- **Detailed information:** Describes further useful information about the concept. We encourage contributors to structure their content by the different aspects they explain, for example, in the case of pages, named parameters, page configuration, available properties, etc. Can contain examples, diagrams, screenshots, and videos.

- **Related topics:** Links to related topics to map out connected information.

Template 4-1 shows the concept topic template of the platformOS Documentation. The part in the beginning is the front matter that includes a Markdown converter for the Liquid pages and metadata like the title and short description for search results. Contributors fill out the information in square brackets based on the instructions.

Template 4-1. The concept topic template of the platformOS Documentation

```
---
converter: markdown
metadata:
  title: "title, NOUN, e.g. Pages"
  description: "short description of the topic, can reuse first
  sentence, max 300 characters"
---
```

[Definition of the concept topic, preferably starting with the title, which answers the question "What is/are [title]?", e.g. "What are pages?". + Brief description related to the concept topic, if applicable.]

[Aspect 1]

[Describe one aspect of the concept topic, e.g. page configuration. Can contain images, diagrams, screenshots, code snippets, but cannot contain step-by-step descriptions of tasks (because those should be separate tutorials).]

[Aspect 2]

Related topics

* [[Link to related topic: concept, tutorial, reference, etc.]()]

Task Topic Template

Task topics describe how to accomplish a task through a series of steps. On a developer documentation site, tutorials (how-to guides) and quickstart guides are of the task topic type.

Quickstart Guides

Quickstart guides target the newcomer audience segment and play an important role in the adoption of your product. As many users learn best by doing, a quickstart guide should include steps that walk the user through the process of completing a task. The guide should be short and simple and list the minimum number of steps required to complete a meaningful task.

Quickstart guides usually have to include information about the domain and introduce domain-related expressions and methods in more detail. It's safest to assume that the user has never before heard of your service.

Tutorials

Tutorials are step-by-step walkthroughs that cover specific tasks developers can do with your product.

Each walkthrough should be the smallest possible chunk that lets the user finish a task. If a process is too complex, break it down into smaller chunks. This makes sure that users can get the help they need without going through steps they're not interested in.

Tutorials teach your users about using your product, so include explanations and link to glossary items, or other content that helps comprehension.

All of your tutorials should follow the same format (as defined in the tutorial template):

- **Title:** Specify the format for the title to keep your documentation consistent and differentiate between different content types.

- **Goal:** What the tutorial helps the user do, what the user will accomplish by the end of the tutorial.

- **Requirements:** What background knowledge or resources the user needs to be able to successfully finish this tutorial.

- **Steps:** Brief overview of the steps in this tutorial.

- **Step 1, Step 2, etc.:** Detailed descriptions of steps, with screenshots, code examples, etc.

- **Next steps:** What the user can do next; if the tutorial is part of a series, link to the next tutorial in the series.

Template 4-2 shows the tutorial template of the platformOS Documentation. We generate the list of steps automatically from third-level headings starting with "Step" and link to each step. In the beginning, we did this manually, and it was part of the tutorial template.

Template 4-2. A task topic template (tutorial) on the platformOS Documentation

```
---
converter: markdown
metadata:
  title: "VERBing a(n)/the NOUN(s)]"
  description: "Short description of the topic, can reuse first
  sentence, max 300 characters"
---

This guide will help you [describe what the user will achieve
by the end of the guide]. [Explain the goal, domain-related
background information, any information that helps understand
the purpose or terminology of the tutorial.]

## Requirements

[List of requirements with links (internal or external) and
explanations where needed.]

- [Requirement 1: explanation if applicable]
- [Requirement 2: explanation if applicable]
- [Requirement 3: explanation if applicable]

## Steps

[optional: purpose of the tutorial/title] is a [number of large
steps, e.g. two]-step process:

<div data-autosteps></div>
```

```
### Step 1: [VERB the/a(n)/your NOUN]
```

```
[Full description of step with additional content, like code
snippet, screenshot, etc.]
```

```
### Step 2: [VERB the/a(n)/your NOUN]
```

```
### Step 3: [VERB the/a(n)/your NOUN]
```

```
## Live example and source code
[optional: link to live site or source code on GitHub]
```

```
## Troubleshooting
[optional: information on fixing issues related to this topic]
```

```
## Additional resources
[optional: bulleted list to additional external resources]
```

```
## Next steps
```

```
Congratulations! You have [what the user has achieved].
[Describe what the user can/has to do next.]
```

```
- [Link to next tutorial or other related topic]()
- [Other link to related topic - if applicable]()
```

Reference Topic Template

Reference topics provide data to support performing a task. They are often displayed as lists or tables. On a developer documentation site, they can describe specifications, parameters, features, and their limitations, but the most often used reference type topic is probably the API reference documentation.

Although the API reference documentation is often auto-generated and follows a formal way of describing a REST API like the OpenAPI Specification, you should still think about how to introduce your API and present data like resource descriptions, endpoints, methods, parameters, and request and response examples.

In the introduction of your API, greet your audience, and explain what the API does, along with some references for requests, HTTP statuses, responses, parameters, limits, and authentication.

Template 4-3 shows a possible outline for the API introduction page.

Template 4-3. Template for the introduction page of an API reference documentation

```
---
converter: markdown
metadata:
  title: "[API name] Introduction"
---

Welcome to the [API name] documentation!

The [API name][api type, e.g. rest] API allows you to [describe
what the API does + test mode, live mode, what you need to get
started, e.g. API key, etc.].

We send information on new additions and changes to our API to
our [mailing list]. Be sure to [subscribe]() to stay informed.

The API documentation starts with a general overview about the
design and technology we implemented, followed by reference
information about specific endpoints.

## Base URL

All URLs referenced in the documentation have the
following base:
[Base URL]

##  Requests
```

[Describe how the API communicates: HTTP, HTTPS, URLs][describe authentication]

Method	Usage
GET	For simple retrieval of information use the GET method. The information you request will be returned to you as a [type of object, e.g. JSON or XML] object.
DELETE	To remove a resource, use the DELETE method. It will remove the object that is specified in the request if it is found. If it is not found, the operation will return a response indicating the object was not available.
PUT	To update information about a resource, use the PUT method.
POST	To create a new object, use the POST method. The POST request needs to contain all the necessary information for creating a new object.
[...]	

HTTP Statuses

Along with the HTTP methods that the API responds to, it also returns standard HTTP statuses, including error codes.
The status contains the error code, while the body of the response usually contains additional information about the problem.

Error code	Meaning

----------------------------------- |
| 200 OK | The request was
successful. |
| 201 CREATED | The request was successful, a new
resource has been created. |
| 204 OK | The request was successful,
the resource specified in the request has been
deleted. |
| 302 FOUND | Redirect response. [...]

                                                               |
| 304 NOT MODIFIED | The resource has not been modified
since the version specified by the respective request headers.
There is no need to retransmit the resource as the client still
has a previously-downloaded copy. |
| 400 BAD REQUEST | The data given in the POST
or PUT failed validation. Explore the response body for
details. |
| 401 UNAUTHORIZED | The supplied credentials,
if any, are not sufficient to create or update the
resource. |
| 404 NOT FOUND | The specified resource could not be
found. |
| 405 METHOD NOT ALLOWED | You can't request POST or PUT
methods to modify the resource. |
| 429 TOO MANY REQUESTS | Your app is sending too many
simultaneous requests to the server. |

| 500 SERVER ERROR | The request has failed
because of server error. Please try to send the request
later. |
| 503 SERVICE UNAVAILABLE | The server is temporarily unable
to respond to the request. Please try to send the request
later. |
```

[Example error response]
```

Responses

When a request is successful, the API sends back a [response
object format, e.g. JSON] object as the response body.
[Optional: exceptions, e.g. DELETE, description of additional
response formats if applicable]

[Other details about responses, e.g keys, meta]

[Explanation of example response]
```

[Example responses:
1. Response for a single object
2. Response for an object collection]
```

Parameters

[Describe how to pass parameters in a request with the API,
e.g. JSON object key-value pairs, query attributes]
```

[Sample object]
```

Limits

[Describe rate limits, e.g. the number of possible API requests with the same OAuth token, rate limiting information in response headers, concurrency rate limiting]

```

[Sample rate limit headers, sample rate exceeded response]
```

Authentication

[Describe ways to authenticate][api keys]

```

[Examples: Authenticate with a bearer authorization header, Authenticate with basic authentication]
```

For describing a REST API, it's practical to follow a predefined standard. Currently, the most widely used standard is the vendor-neutral OpenAPI Specification[14]. Following a standard allows you to programmatically parse and display information. You can find a detailed description of the OpenAPI Specification and many examples in its public GitHub repository.

Writing API documentation is a specific area of technical writing, so it helps to have at least one technical writer on your team who is experienced in writing docs for APIs.

---

[14]https://swagger.io/specification/

Tip   If you'd like to learn more about writing documentation for APIs, I recommend you to delve into Tom Johnson's course Documenting APIs: A guide for technical writers and engineers[15].

Practically, you can start by writing an introduction page and documentation for your API and generating the reference using a tool like Swagger. Then, invite members of your team and community to use the documentation and provide feedback. With a couple of user research rounds and iterations, you can build usable API documentation relatively quickly. Note all findings for the reference topic format and any helpful links for contributors in your documentation style guide.

Documentation Style Guide Checklist

This checklist summarizes my recommendations for the elements of a minimum viable developer documentation style guide. Feel free to use it as an inspiration for your own documentation style guide, for planning, or for tracking your progress.

- Introduction: Goal of the style guide, what it includes
- Detailed description of the audience, personas included
- Writing guidelines
  - Language and spelling
  - Tone
  - Present tense
  - Second person
  - Active voice

---

[15]https://idratherbewriting.com/learnapidoc/

- Capitalization

  - Punctuation

  - Numbers

- Lists

- Format

- Formatting guidelines

  - Headings

  - Code examples

  - Tables

  - Paths

- Images

- Videos

- Accessibility

- Inclusive language

- Templates for topic types

  - Task

  - Concept

  - Reference

Changelogs and Release Notes

Changelogs provide a comprehensive and detailed chronological list of changes to your product predominantly aimed at developers, while release notes communicate these changes in a more readable way for a wider target audience. No matter which format – or both – you choose based on the needs of your community (which you understood through user research), they are valuable and necessary ways to communicate product changes to your users and possibly open dialogues with your community about where your product is going.

We found that publishing release notes in a chronological order works well for the platformOS community, so we specified a format that includes the following information about each release:

- New features

- Improvements

- Fixes

Each section lists items in bullet points.

Template 4-4 shows the structure of release notes we write and publish on the platformOS Documentation.

Template 4-4. Release note template for the platformOS Documentation

```
---
converter: markdown
metadata:
  title: [main points listed, sentence case]
  description: [Month DD, YYYY]
  skip_contribute_button: true
  last_edit: false
slug: release-notes/DD-MONTH-YYYY
---

#### {{ page.metadata.description }}

<h4 class="release-note release-note__improved">NEW</h4>

* [**New feature 1**: short description of new feature, link to
documentation if applicable]
```

```
* [**New feature n**: short description of new feature, link to
documentation if applicable]

<h4 class="release-note release-note__improved">IMPROVED</h4>

* [**Improvement 1**: short description of improvement]
* [**Improvement n**: short description of improvement]

<h4 class="release-note release-note__fixed">FIXED</h4>

* [**Fix 1**: short description of fix]
* [**Fix n**: short description of fix]
```

Use Cases

Use cases describe interactions between the user and the system to accomplish a specific task. Use cases tell users how to obtain the end result. They usually address a technical audience and focus on the problem and the solution, so they should include detailed descriptions of the technical implementation and code examples. Our community always appreciates new use cases and actively contributes to this section of our documentation site.

Template 4-5 shows the format we defined for use cases. It helps contributors clearly describe the problem, the challenges they faced, the solution they developed, and the results they achieved.

Template 4-5. Template for use cases on the platformOS Documentation

```
---
converter: markdown
metadata:
  title: "VERBing a(n)/the NOUN(s) [title case, e.g. Recording
  Your Terminal to SVG]"
```

Description: "This use case describes [short description of
the use case, e.g. how we recorded a terminal window and
saved it as an SVG to embed it on our marketing website]."

This use case describes [description of your use case, add any
background information needed for understanding].

Problem [or Situation, if the word problem doesn't fit]

[
- Describe the problem you wanted to solve
- Describe any additional factors related to the problem (e.g.
  performance considerations)
]

Challenges
[
- Describe what made the problem tricky to solve
- Describe any trials and errors
]

Solution
[
- Describe how you solved the problem
- Describe why you chose that solution
- Add how platformOS was helpful in solving the problem, which
  features you used
- Add code examples
- Add links to platformOS documentation where applicable
- Mention industry specific best practices where applicable
]

Results
[

- Describe or show your solution, e.g. demo site, link to module, etc.
- Add screenshots, images, diagrams where applicable
- Add a video where you explain the process and the result if you'd like to

Author information
[
- Author name
- Author position
- Author bio (short)
- Company name
- Link to website/code repository
]

Legal Copy

Your developer documentation site will also need some copy to cover your stance on legal issues. As a minimum, you should have the following:

- A valid **copyright notice** for your site that includes the copyright symbol ©, or the word "Copyright" or "Copr.", the year of publication, and the name of the copyright owner.

- A **license** that explains the terms of use. If your documentation is open source, you can quote from and link to an open source license.

- A **disclaimer** that explains that you try to ensure that all content and code included in your documentation are up to date and error-free but could include technical, typographical, or other general errors and can change without notice.

Developer Onboarding

A good onboarding process educates developers about your product, boosts engagement, and improves product adoption. Your onboarding will probably arch through different channels (like registration interfaces, sandboxes, webinars, etc.), but a significant portion of it will reside on your documentation site. Content-wise, your onboarding is very similar to any other part of your site: it includes different types of topics, examples, images, videos, and so on. You should also follow the same iterative process of carrying out user research, validating your assumptions, creating content, and then testing and adjusting it in multiple rounds.

Based on our experience, one of the biggest challenges is to define onboarding routes for different target audience segments and skill levels. To date, we have developed three main onboarding journeys for the three main segments of our target audience:

- **Nontechnical users** can click through an intuitive and simple setup wizard, create a demo site, and install a module in minutes.

- **Semitechnical users** can create a sandbox in which they can experiment by cloning a demo site from our GitHub repository. They also have the option to go through our Get Started guides starting from the beginning.

- **Technical users** can follow a more complex tutorial that walks them through the steps of creating an app on platformOS, such as setting up their development environment, syncing with GitHub, deploying and testing their apps, and more. It explains basic concepts, including giving insights into the main building blocks and the logic behind our product while also giving recommendations on best practice workflows.

A similar approach could work for developer documentation sites with a large difference in skill levels between the main personas.

Developing your onboarding is similar to developing any other content for your site: you can work closely with a UX researcher, use all the methods and tools described in this book, and iteratively improve your user experience – just be aware that onboarding is a large area on its own that will need your attention and involvement from many of your team members over a longer period of time.

Search Engine Optimization

Search engine optimization (SEO) is essential for enhancing the visibility of your documentation site and boosting its credibility. It's not just about driving traffic; it's about delivering the right content to the right audience at the right time. If your content is optimized effectively for search engines, it is more likely to rank highly for specific topic searches, transforming your site into a trusted resource.

As a basic requirement for SEO, ensure that each piece of content on your documentation site follows these guidelines:

- **Title:** Each page should have a unique <title> element. Craft a well-defined title tag to enable search engines to understand your page content and help users decide whether your page is relevant to their search query.

- **Meta description:** Provide a concise summary of your content that can drive clicks from search engine results pages.

- **Descriptive link text:** Utilize descriptive link texts to enhance user comprehension, improve SEO, and promote better accessibility.

- **Alt tags for images:** Use alt tags correctly to make your images more accessible to users with visual impairments and to provide valuable context to search engines.

The guidelines and templates discussed in this chapter focus on creating well-structured, high-quality content that is not only easy for users to navigate and understand but also optimized for SEO.

Summary

This chapter dealt with the practicalities of producing content for your developer documentation site, such as

- Choosing a markup language

- Writing a documentation style guide

- Creating templates for different content types

- Thinking about additional content you need

- Preparing content for onboarding different personas

- Following some basic SEO best practices

After so much planning, research, and preparation, it's time to start implementing your documentation site.

CHAPTER 5

Implementation

You laid a solid foundation for building your developer documentation by gaining an empathetic understanding of the needs of your target audience, planning your editorial workflow, and outlining the structure of your content. This chapter discusses how all these elements fall into place in the technical implementation when you'll create wireframes, implement a design, develop the code base, and set up a deployment process.

Wireframes

A wireframe is a low-fidelity visual representation of the layout and structure of your website that outlines the placement and hierarchy of key elements such as navigation menus, content blocks, images, and other interactive elements.

Following the Content First approach, examining your content needs, and creating templates provide you with a thorough understanding of the structure of the content you want to display. These templates can not only be used to support contribution and ensure consistency, they also help you identify the importance of each UI element and create wireframes for most of your content. For example, your UX team can create a first version wireframe for tutorials by creating each element in the tutorial template in a wireframe software; then you can collect feedback on it from your team and users and adjust the wireframes as needed.

© Diana Lakatos 2023
D. Lakatos, *Crafting Docs for Success*, Design Thinking,
https://doi.org/10.1007/978-1-4842-9594-6_5

Figure 5-1 shows some initial wireframes we created for the platformOS Documentation.

Figure 5-1. *Wireframes of the platformOS Documentation*

Figure 5-2 shows the first wireframe we created for the tutorial content type of the platformOS Documentation in Balsamiq[1]. Once we finalized the templates and produced some initial content, we had everything we needed to start thinking about the layouts of different pages. We approached this process just like we approached other aspects of our documentation, so "final" templates mean "final for now but can be tweaked later." We used what we've learned about our personas from the first phase and collected patterns to identify how to best serve our audience. That helped us create the first wireframes that we iterated based on team feedback. We created wireframes for each layout in Balsamiq and collaborated on them in Marvel[2]. Balsamiq is a rapid wireframing tool used for creating low-fidelity wireframes for software or website layouts. Marvel is a design platform for rapid prototyping, testing, and handoff.

---

[1]https://balsamiq.com/
[2]https://marvelapp.com/

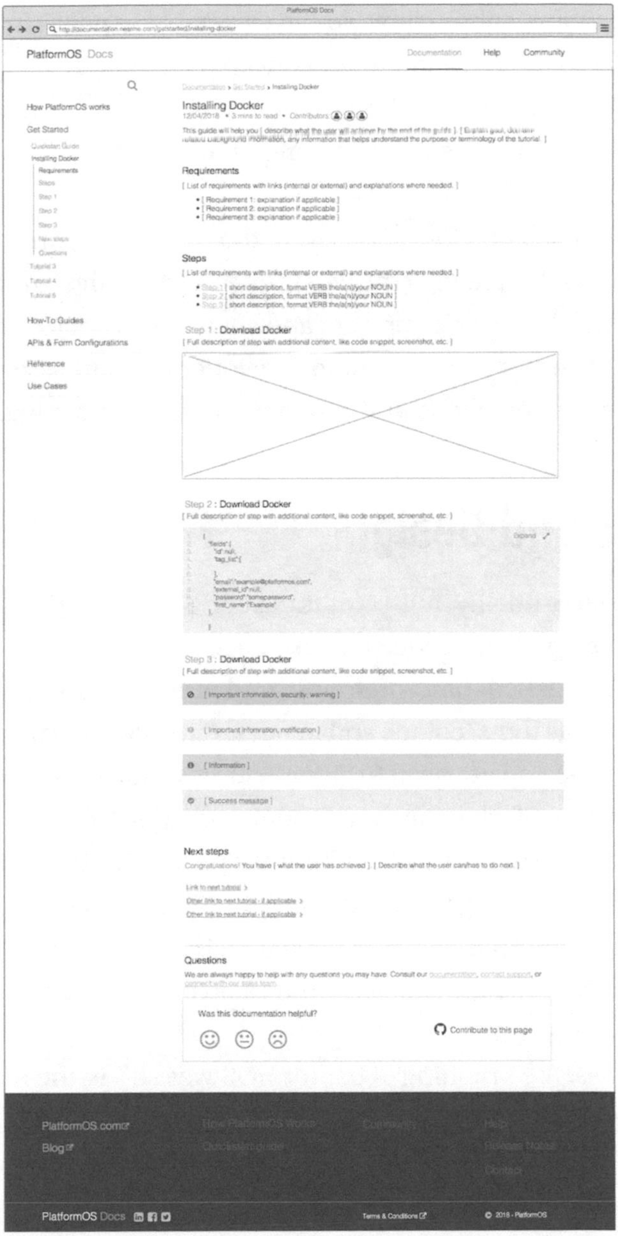

Figure 5-2. *The first version of the tutorial content type's wireframe created for the platformOS Documentation*

We also thought about how we can evolve these pages in the future and created separate wireframes or concepts for later development phases. This helped us plan our site development process. As always, we heavily relied on user feedback, so we were prepared to iteratively adjust our layouts.

We now use Figma[3] for every part of the UX, design, and collaboration process: not just for creating the wireframes and the designs based on the wireframes, but we also present and share our work to other team members or to users, hand it over to developers, export assets, provide feedback, version our work, and create prototypes for testing.

Layouts and Design

Layouts are high-fidelity, full-color mockups or designs that show what the website or application will look like once it is built. Layouts are more detailed and polished than wireframes and often include specific design elements such as fonts, colors, and images. Layouts are typically created after wireframes and are used to give clients and stakeholders a more complete picture of what the final product will look like.

As you have probably noticed from the process described so far, I advocate for prioritizing the audience, content, and user experience before visual design. This approach is aligned with both the Design Thinking and Content First methodologies, which also emphasize deferring visual design to a later stage.

In our case, the branding of platformOS was still in the making when we were working on the wireframes and implementation. By the time our branding was done, we had a working documentation site tested with real users and continuously improved based on relevant feedback. We believe

---

[3]https://www.figma.com/

that this way we could focus on the most important aspects for each phase, and our documentation site had a solid foundation that the design could enhance.

To allow for enough focus on user needs and usability, I recommend going with a minimal, functional design for your first version that looks and works well and is in sync with your brand. After publishing the first version of your documentation, you will collect a lot of feedback, learn even more about your audience, and find many ways to adjust and improve your docs including the design that you wouldn't have been able to arrive at without sharing the first version.

Figure 5-3 shows how the visuals of the platformOS Documentation's homepage have changed. We have continuously updated the layouts, navigation, and content and had a visual design update each year in the first three years.

Figure 5-3. *Design changes on the platformOS Documentation homepage in the first three years*

We created the first functional design based on our initial UX research and by going through the Design Thinking process. Then, we had a year of iterations and fine-tuning with this minimal design and then changed to the second design.

At this point, the platformOS branding had been prepared, but we haven't tested it or applied it to the Web yet; this was the first design that followed our branding.

While we were happily using the second design, we started fine-tuning our branding and creating the Design Systems for platformOS sites. We also had a full design update on our marketing site, and during all of this, we got an understanding of how we would like to use our branding online. We kept the clean look and feel that is helpful on a documentation site but added the elements from our branding to enhance the platformOS feel.

Although we didn't use a Design System when we created the layouts for the platformOS Documentation, now we use at least a Style Guide and Component Library for all of our projects. The process now starts with creating the style guide based on the brand defined colors and fonts. Then, we work with the Atomic Design methodology to create the layouts from the bottom up by building the smallest components like buttons, links, and fields and then combining them to create larger, more complex components. The Atomic Design methodology consists of five stages, which are as follows:

1. **Atoms** are the smallest building blocks of UI elements, such as buttons, icons, labels, and inputs.

2. **Molecules** are combinations of atoms that create more complex UI elements, such as forms, search bars, and navigation menus.

3. **Organisms** are combinations of molecules that create even more complex UI elements, such as headers, footers, and product listings.

4. **Templates** are the final layouts that bring together all the organisms, molecules, and atoms to create specific pages or views within an application or website.

5. **Pages** are the final product, where the templates are filled with real content to create a complete user interface.

We usually add documentation related to the components right in the Figma file. Working from a Design System with reusable and modular components, which can be combined in different ways to create a wide variety of designs, helps your designers and developers create consistent, efficient, and scalable designs that are easier to maintain and update over time. The specific elements included in your Design System will be dictated by your particular requirements, team structure, and product range. At platformOS, Design Systems start with a Style Guide and a Component Library. The Style Guide forms the foundation of the system, outlining colors, typography, and design tokens. Adhering to the Atomic Design methodology, these styles are incorporated by the Component Library, which facilitates the creation of Sections and Modules, subsequently informing Page templates. Additionally, the Design System features Getting Started and Rules pages, offering users crucial information. If we started developing our documentation now, we would use a Design System, and our plan is to use one as part of the next larger design update of our site.

Following an iterative process where you share your wireframes and designs with users, collect their feedback, analyze the data, and prioritize planned changes ensures that you are conscious of the reasons for each design change, which in turn helps you

- Avoid any unnecessary changes that could lead to increased complexity, confusion, and inconsistency in the user interface

- Focus on the needs and expectations of your users so you can come up with solutions that address real user pain points and improve the user experience

- Measure the impact of the change on the user experience and validate the effectiveness of the change and make further improvements if necessary

- Save time and resources by prioritizing your efforts and making the most of your design team's resources

Although I discussed design as a separate topic, it can be closely connected to the technical implementation that you choose. Many solutions have design templates that you can apply and customize, or allow you to create your own themes.

Technical Implementation

In the discovery phase, you could lean on your UX researcher and UX designer team members; then, your technical writers took over when you were working on the editorial workflow, style guide, and templates. UXers then created wireframes, and designers crafted layouts for all pages. All throughout, your developer team members actively participated and contributed to finding the best solutions for a largely developer audience. Now is the time for the developer team to get coding and implement all that you have planned together.

There are several options for implementing a developer documentation site.

Document hosting platforms like Read the Docs[4], GitBook[5], and SwaggerHub[6] provide pre-built templates for creating developer documentation sites. They also offer integrations with popular development tools like GitHub, Bitbucket[7], and GitLab.

Static site generators like Jekyll[8], Hugo[9], Gatsby[10], and Sphinx[11] can be used to generate documentation sites from Markdown files. They offer a simple and fast way to create static sites with good performance.

Content management systems can also be used to create developer documentation sites. We built our documentation site on our own product, platformOS, which is a **Platform-as-a-Service** solution.

And as always, you can go with a **custom-built solution**, but given the wide range of tools and solutions available, you will probably be able to find an existing solution that fulfills your requirements or at least one that you can use as a starting point and tweak it to fit your needs.

Each option has its own pros and cons, depending on the size and complexity of your project. The best option for your project will depend on your specific needs and requirements. In this section, I explore some approaches to give you an idea of the different routes you can go, but to select a solution, you will probably need to examine solutions in more detail.

Regardless of which approach you follow, you will need a way to check what your site looks like before it goes live. You can build your docs locally, but ideally, you should have a staging environment that displays your site

---

[4]https://www.figma.com/

[5]https://www.gitbook.com/

[6]https://swagger.io/tools/swaggerhub/

[7]https://bitbucket.org

[8]https://jekyllrb.com/

[9]https://gohugo.io/

[10]https://www.gatsbyjs.com/

[11]https://www.sphinx-doc.org/

exactly as it will look like on production. Staging is great for checking your work periodically as you edit, conduct reviews, and show the pages if you need approvals from management or leadership.

Git

To build a Docs-as-Code workflow, you will have to become intimately familiar with Git, a free and open source distributed version control system. Git and tools leveraging it like GitHub or GitLab can be the underpinning of your whole technical implementation. Chapter 3, "Editorial Workflow," explained a Docs-as-Code workflow implemented on GitHub in detail, so here I'd like to add some more considerations and approaches you can leverage Git for.

Although it's not part of a Docs-as-Code workflow, you can use GitHub wikis to take notes and draft documentation in the early stages of development. We use wikis to take notes on modules that are in development and share them with our community to get their feedback as early as possible.

As the most basic example of a Docs-as-Code workflow, you can use GitHub to store and edit your website content and GitHub Pages[12] to publish your site.

There are many Git clients available for different operating systems that provide a user-friendly interface for managing Git repositories like GitHub Desktop or Sourcetree. They allow your contributors to find the tool they are most comfortable with: they can choose to use Git from the command line, through a graphical user interface, or even through a code editor that includes built-in Git integration like Visual Studio Code.

---

[12]https://pages.github.com/

Tip   If you're interested in exploring Git further, I recommend *Beginning Git and GitHub* by Mariot Tsitoara[13]. It's a comprehensive guide to version control, project management, and teamwork, primarily written for a beginner developer audience, but it's also useful for noncoders and writers.

Static Site Generators

Static site generators allow developers to create websites that are composed of static files, like HTML, CSS, and JavaScript. These files are generated by the site generator from a set of templates and content files and are then deployed to a web server and displayed to users. Static site generators pre-generate all the content at build time, which means that the content can be served more quickly and with less server resources. They usually provide a web server preview, so when you are editing your site locally, you can check all your changes in a browser before even pushing them to the staging environment.

Static site generators are a good choice for websites that have relatively simple content and design requirements such as documentation sites. You can write your content in Markdown or HTML and flexibly use pre-made templates, custom code, or JavaScript libraries to extend the functionality of your site or improve its design.

Static sites are incredibly fast since they only serve pre-generated files, so there is no need for a server to generate content on the fly. This means that static sites can handle large amounts of traffic without experiencing performance issues, which in turn improves user experience and sustainability.

---

[13]https://www.amazon.com/Beginning-Git-GitHub-Comprehensive-Management/dp/1484253124

As they don't rely on a database or server-side code, static sites are less susceptible to security vulnerabilities such as SQL injection attacks or cross-site scripting attacks.

Static sites are highly scalable by leveraging a content delivery network (CDN), which caches the pre-generated files and serves them to users from a network of servers around the world. This means that static sites can handle large amounts of traffic without the need for complex server infrastructure.

Open source static site generators have a community of developers who contribute additional functionality and themes. Themes are pre-designed templates that you can use to quickly set up the visual design and layout of your website. Many themes specifically created for documentation sites are also available online, both free and paid. As they are customizable, you can choose one that mostly fits your needs and recolor or reconfigure them for your brand or specific requirements.

Additionally to all these benefits, there is one more aspect that makes static site generators a great choice for implementing developer documentation sites. You can store your files in a code repository (e.g., on GitHub) and build them directly from the repository, so static site generators are inherently suitable to implement Docs-as-Code workflows.

There are hundreds of static site generators available for a wide range of different uses, like blogs, personal websites, portfolios, and so on. You can check a list of static site generators on `http://jamstack.org/generators`. You can order the generators by GitHub stars, so you can get some insight about their popularity. Although choosing a popular static site generator usually has the benefits of more available resources, themes, and a more active community, popularity should not be the only factor you take into consideration when selecting a solution for your developer documentation. Look for static site generators that provide the functionality you need in your developer documentation site based on the needs of your target audience you identified in earlier stages of the planning and development process. Some popular static site generators used to build documentation sites include Jekyll, Hugo, MkDocs[14], Gatsby, Docusaurus, and Sphinx.

Jekyll is a popular static site generator originally written by the co-founder of GitHub in the Ruby programming language. It uses a simple file-based structure to organize the content of your website. You create pages and posts using Markdown, but Jekyll also supports Liquid, a template engine that enables you to create reusable templates for your website's layout and design. It also supports plug-ins, which can be used to extend its functionality and add new features. Some common Jekyll plug-ins include those for generating sitemaps, optimizing images, and integrating with social media platforms.

A built-in development server allows you to preview your website locally before publishing it.

Many hosting services like GitHub Pages offer built-in support for Jekyll, and (using a plug-in) you can also choose to publish your site to AWS S3.

Hugo is a fast and modern static site generator written in the Go programming language that offers a wide range of features and configuration options, including support for multilingual content, taxonomies, and content types. It also supports shortcodes, which allow you to add complex functionality to your pages without having to write custom HTML or JavaScript code. Hugo supports live reloading, which means that you can see changes to your website in real time as you make them. Additionally to providing all the usual features of a static site generator, Hugo sets itself apart from other generators by being one of the fastest and most efficient options available, thanks to its use of Go's concurrency and parallelism features.

Jekyll and Hugo have probably the largest communities, which ensures you can easily find support if you need help with your project or would like to delve deeper into working with these static site generators.

---

[14]https://www.mkdocs.org/

MkDocs is a Python-based static site generator specifically designed for documentation projects that you might know through one of its themes, ReadtheDocs, which resembles the Read the Docs platform. One of the main benefits of MkDocs is its built-in support for the Material Design framework that allows you to create modern and responsive websites. MkDocs also includes a range of built-in themes and extensions that can be used to add additional functionality, such as syntax highlighting or table of contents. You can add search like Algolia to any static site generator, but with its focus on documentation, MkDocs has built-in search. It provides a built-in development server for preview and a command to deploy to GitHub Pages.

Gatsby is a static site generator built on top of the React framework that also offers a cloud-hosted version. As it's suited to build web applications, it's more complex than the static site generators I discussed before. Gatsby includes a wide range of built-in features and plug-ins that can be used to add functionality to your website. These include support for GraphQL, which allows you to query your data sources using a single language and API, and a plug-in architecture that makes it easy to integrate with other tools and services. For a simple documentation site, you might want to go with another static site generator, but if you are planning to build a more complex developer portal, Gatsby can be a good choice. Redocly, for example, provides a sample starter developer portal built in Gatsby.

Docusaurus is an open source React-based static site generator used for building documentation websites. It was created by Facebook and is currently maintained by a community of developers. It provides blog support, internationalization, search, and versioning.

Sphinx is a Python-based static site generator that is integrated with Read the Docs. Designed specifically as a documentation tool, it provides features like robust search, linking to sections, automating titles based on links, cross-references, and other advanced linking. It also supports the use of reStructuredText.

Tip   For step-by-step tutorials on setting up various static site generators and integrating them with a CI/CD system, I recommend checking out the learning resources at `www.docslikecode.com/learn`.

If you have an API that you want to publish documentation for, along with static site generators and other documentation solutions, you should look into tools for generating the API reference as well.

API Documentation Generators

API documentation generators provide various features to help you create comprehensive, easy-to-understand documentation for your APIs. Here are some common features you should be looking for when selecting an API documentation generator:

- **Automatic documentation generation:** Automatically generate documentation for your API from its source code or from an OpenAPI specification file.

- **Code examples:** Include code examples in various programming languages to help developers understand how to use the API.

- **Interactive documentation:** Many API documentation generators offer interactive documentation that allows developers to try out the API's endpoints and see the responses in real time.

- **Test requests:** Some API documentation generators allow developers to send test requests directly from the documentation to see how the API responds.

- **Search:** Allow developers to quickly find the documentation they need.

- **Customization:** Customize the look and feel of the documentation, including colors, fonts, and logos.

- **Versioning:** Support versioning, making it easy to maintain and document changes to the API over time.

- **Integration with other tools:** Many API documentation generators integrate with other development tools, such as testing frameworks and code editors.

There are several tools available for generating API reference documentation, for example:

- **SwaggerHub:** A cloud-based platform for designing, building, and documenting APIs using the OpenAPI specification. It provides a collaborative environment for teams to work on API projects, with features such as version control, team management, integration with popular development tools, and automatic documentation generation.

- **Redocly[15]:** An open source tool for generating API documentation from OpenAPI specifications. It provides a customizable interface for viewing and interacting with API documentation and supports a variety of OpenAPI features, including endpoint descriptions, parameters, response codes, and security definitions. It also includes features for customizing the documentation layout and appearance, such as changing the color scheme and adding custom CSS.

---

[15]https://redocly.com/

- **Stoplight**[16]**:** A platform for designing, documenting, and testing APIs that includes a tool for generating API documentation. The REST API and OpenAPI documentation generator provided by Stoplight offers various options for your API consumers to experiment with your APIs, like test requests or code examples in many different programming languages.

Tip   You can learn more about API documentation generators and try them out as you follow the course I previously recommended, Documenting APIs: A guide for technical writers and engineers[17] by Tom Johnson.

As the features, availability, and popularity of different static site generators and API documentation generators can change over time, I recommend you to ask your developers, listen to industry experts, and read recent articles that list and explore the most popular solutions as a starting point for your own research.

platformOS

As a large portion of my experience and the examples in this book come from working on the platformOS Documentation, I will briefly describe the technical implementation of our documentation site.

Our documentation site is built on platformOS, and we store the code base and content files in a public GitHub repository. We are now also working on combining platformOS with GitHub and a static site generator to build a solution for quickly implementing documentation sites that follow the Docs-as-Code methodology and the editorial workflow we

---

[16]https://stoplight.io/
[17]https://idratherbewriting.com/learnapidoc

use. Besides standard web technologies like HTML, CSS, and JavaScript (including JSON and AJAX), we use a couple of languages like YAML, Liquid, and GraphQL in our code.

Automation

When you follow a Docs-as-Code approach, you build the documentation automatically after the editing and review phase and then publish the changes without much manual intervention through a continuous integration and continuous deployment (CI/CD) workflow. You can include automated tests that help you catch errors before deploying the site to the production environment.

CI/CD

Continuous integration (CI) means that code is continuously tested, integrated with other code changes, and merged. Continuous deployment or continuous delivery (CD) means that code is continuously deployed with each patch to the entire code base. For documentation, CI/CD means that when you edit content and merge it to the Git repository of your production site, it triggers the publication process: it builds your site, runs tests, and deploys it to the live environment.

Utilizing CI/CD for a developer documentation site helps with frequent and fast releases, which are needed for keeping your docs up to date, fixing errors, and working with quick iterations and feedback cycles.

Contributors can edit one or multiple files, and the changes will be automatically published. They can work concurrently, and the version control system will notify them if there is a part of the documentation they both edited at the same time (called a conflict) before they could merge the changes. They can resolve the conflict by selecting the version to be published or editing the content further.

In the event of an issue with the documentation site, CI/CD enables developers to easily roll back to a previous version.

Figure 5-4 shows the steps of the CI/CD workflow of the platformOS Documentation. Our documentation has a staging environment for development and testing and a production environment which is the live site where changes are deployed if all tests are green. On every code merge to our main branch, our CI/CD of choice, GitHub Actions, runs quality checks to ensure that the website will remain operational after the changes are deployed.

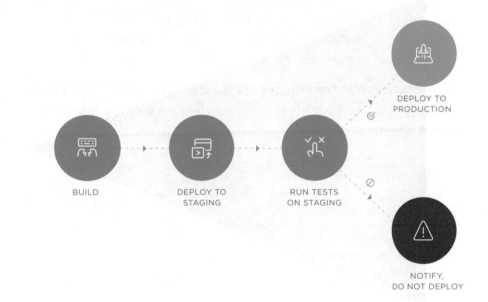

Figure 5-4. *Steps of the CI/CD process of the platformOS Documentation*

Tests

Automated testing is a key part of the CI/CD process, which helps to ensure that the documentation site works and looks as intended after the changes have been deployed.

For example, these are the steps in our test process in order:

1. The system tests build assets and our auto-generated GraphQL documentation.

2. It deploys the project to the staging environment using our command-line interface tool.

3. It runs end-to-end tests using CodeceptJS.

4. It runs Google Lighthouse to catch possible performance regressions. This is the step where you can run accessibility checkers, inclusive language linters, or any other checkers and linters.

If everything went according to our standards, it deploys to production. Figure 5-5 shows the steps of the testing process for the platformOS Documentation.

1. BUILD ASSETS   **2.** DEPLOY TO STAGING   **3.** RUN E2E TESTS   **4.** RUN LIGHTHOUSE

STEP 1   **STEP 2**   **STEP 3**   **STEP 4**

Builds assets (webpack,   Deploy project to the   Run end-to-end tests   Run Google Lighthouse
Tailwind CSS), GraphQL   staging environment   (CodeceptJS).   and other checkers and
documentation.   using the pos-cli.   linters.

Figure 5-5. *The testing process of the platformOS Documentation*

Many types of tests can be included; for example, you can test for broken links. We also experimented with including a grammar checker in the test phase but found that it didn't work consistently. It flagged some content as incorrect when it was not, and the other way around, it also missed some errors. In the end, we decided to remove it.

Including automated testing is one way to ensure good documentation quality, but I will discuss many more in Chapter 10, "Measures of Success."

Summary

This chapter walked you through the steps of implementing a developer documentation site by

- Creating wireframes for the most used content types and other pages like your homepage

- Creating layouts based on the wireframes

- Exploring technologies for the implementation like Git, static site generators, and API documentation generators

- Learning about automating the deployment process using a CI/CD workflow and automated tests

Now that you have an idea of how to build a working developer documentation site, let's discuss how you can help contributors have the best experience and add the most value.

CHAPTER 6

Community

One of the approaches discussed in Chapter 1, "Approaches," is **community-driven documentation**, which refers to a collaborative approach to documentation development where you aim to involve your users in all stages of the process. This approach encourages open communication and transparency between the documentation team and the community, allowing for early feedback, testing, and validation of assumptions. As community members are actively involved in the documentation process, providing input, contributing content, and helping to shape the direction of the documentation, the resulting documentation becomes more user centered and relevant to the community's needs.

This chapter discusses how to make it easy and enjoyable for your users to contribute and what communication channels you can use to share information and have conversations with your users and touches upon building a community where everyone feels respected and included.

Contribution

When I talk about contribution, I always start with emphasizing that every input from your team, users, clients, business partners, and sometimes even from individuals with vastly different areas of expertise that changes, improves, or moves your documentation forward can be considered contribution. In this sense, writing content is only a small portion of all contributions to the documentation.

© Diana Lakatos 2023
D. Lakatos, *Crafting Docs for Success*, Design Thinking,
https://doi.org/10.1007/978-1-4842-9594-6_6

Ways to Contribute

When the platformOS Documentation won the UK Technical Communication Awards in 2019, the judges highlighted this collaborative aspect of the community-driven documentation approach in their feedback:

> *"This is an outstanding example of how technical product documentation can work as an integrated part of the product, the teams that create it and the community that uses it. The technical communication 'team' is everyone in the business and many out in the partner and user communities. But the only way that 'team' can produce the quality they have is through strong leadership driving through a carefully considered strategy."*

Everyone in the platformOS team and many members of our community are involved in writing content, providing feedback, and improving the site.

- Developers provide information and code examples for technical writers in the form of drafts, descriptions, or videos.

- Account managers and other team members interacting with clients share details about where more support would be needed and write drafts themselves.

- Developers and designers in our team work on making our developer portal a high-performance site with great usability facilitating the results of our UX research and feedback.

- Community contributors provide feedback, patches, and new content to our documentation.

- External contributors review and edit our documentation to suggest changes or improve clarity.

As the leader of a documentation project, I think it's very helpful to think of yourself as someone who is steering the project in the right direction, instead of trying to control every aspect of it. Use objective research to collect the information you need, get to know your audience, and build documentation that best serves their needs based on the knowledge you gained.

Creating a mindset where the exchange of information and ideas is the foundation of the work we are doing helped us in more ways than we initially expected.

First of all, we could always be sure that what we are working on is needed. This saved us a lot of time and money in the long run. If you have an idea, share it with your community first. If it turns out that your users would love it, you can start working on it knowing that you're providing value. If they don't like or need it, let it go, and work on something that improves their experience.

Constant collaboration builds trust. We built strong relationships with many members of our community through conducting user research, discussing their feedback on various channels, and reviewing content they contributed.

The feedback they provided not only shaped our documentation but often contributed to the development of our product: when a part of the documentation is not clear, or a process is difficult to follow, always investigate whether the documentation needs some adjustments or the process, UI, or UX of the product needs to be improved.

Some ways community members can contribute:

- Participating in various types of user research at all phases of your documentation development process

- Testing your documentation and reporting errors

- Providing feedback on documentation topics, pointing out processes that are difficult to follow, asking for missing information

- Providing feedback on your editorial workflow, where they get stuck, what they would need to make it easier

- Participating in discussions about your future plans, helping you prioritize

- Participating in discussions with other community members, helping newcomers

- Editing documentation topics, fixing typos, adding missing information, removing outdated information

- Writing documentation topics, providing use cases

- Reviewing documentation topics others have written

- Providing feedback on your communication, what they need more information on, what channels work for them

When you are thinking about your contributors, make sure to consider the largest possible group of people who you think could contribute and create opportunities for all of them. Three major areas of contribution I'll explore in more detail are providing feedback, editing and writing content, and participating in user research.

Feedback

Every time you communicate with your users, or watch them communicate with each other, you might receive feedback that you can use to improve your documentation.

Users often post questions to your team or other users on various channels when they can't find answers in the documentation. In these cases, be sure to enhance the relevant documentation topic with the answer to their question. This way, other users will readily find the information they seek.

Work closely with your support team; they know where users struggle with your product. You can use this information to improve specific aspects of your product, your documentation, or both.

Pay attention to questions and issues that come up multiple times, and dedicate time and resources to prioritize writing or updating the documentation for them.

Keep track of all the feedback you receive in a consistent and sustainable way. We open a GitHub issue for each piece of feedback we would like to discuss further or act on.

Feedback on Documentation Topics

The feedback you receive through various channels is quite varied as it can relate to different features of your product, your documentation structure, navigation, content, contribution, search, and so on. To collect feedback more precisely, we added a feedback block at the bottom of each documentation page on the platformOS Documentation, where the minimum input is clicking on a smiley indicator, but users can answer a question and share their suggestions, too.

Figure 6-1 shows the feedback block on the platformOS Documentation. It asks users to provide more information based on the smiley they clicked:

- **Happy smiley:** We're glad you liked our documentation page! Why did you like it? How could we make it even better?

- **Neutral smiley:** We are continuously working on our docs to make them better. How do you think we could improve this page?

- **Sad smiley:** We're sorry you didn't like our documentation page. What was the problem? How do you think we could fix it?

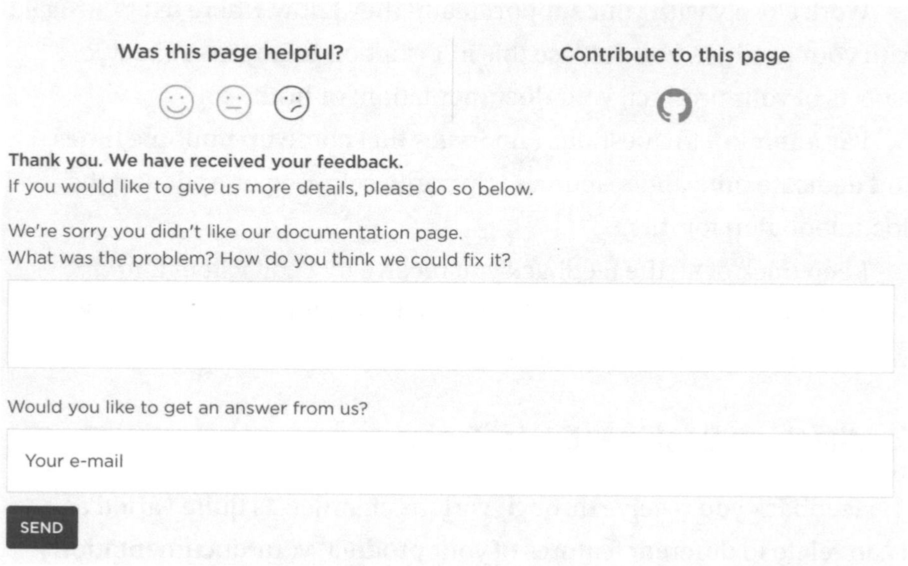

Was this page helpful?

Contribute to this page

Thank you. We have received your feedback.
If you would like to give us more details, please do so below.

We're sorry you didn't like our documentation page.
What was the problem? How do you think we could fix it?

Would you like to get an answer from us?

Your e-mail

SEND

Figure 6-1. *The feedback block on the platformOS Documentation*

The feedback block worked very well for us because the notifications we receive include the topic the user gave feedback on along with their assessment, and most of the time users add some explanation of the problem or an idea for improvement, too. Notifications from the feedback block clearly show which topics need more attention.

Although this tool is very useful for collecting feedback on specific documentation topics, it can't be used to collect feedback on the documentation in general (navigation, structure, etc.), or to measure documentation quality. We also knew not to use this tool for analytics, as the results would be heavily skewed: users are more likely to report issues than commenting on documentation that fulfilled their expectations, which is very useful when you are looking for input on how to improve your docs.

Content Contribution

Another large area of contribution – the one that usually comes to mind when you hear about documentation contributors – is content contribution.

Content contribution comes in many forms, too: fixing typos, making small edits or large rewrites, or submitting new content. For some quick editing, like fixing typos or adding links, contributors can edit the content on the GitHub UI. This also works well for less technical contributors. We display a "Contribute to this page" button on each documentation topic that opens the topic in the GitHub editor.

For heavy editing, adding new content, or developers who prefer to use git, you can provide a complete Docs-as-Code workflow.

On the platformOS Documentation, most of our authors are at least semitechnical. Less technical users sometimes provide use cases, where we help them by providing a use case template in Google Docs format instead of Markdown if needed. We go through the review and editing in Google Docs if that makes the experience more comfortable for them. After the content is finalized in Google Docs, our technical writers refine it and convert it into Markdown format. They then send a pull request, and the content proceeds through the remainder of the editorial workflow just like any other content.

Another aspect that you have to consider as an international team and community is the different language skills and writing skills of your contributors.

A style guide and templates help a lot. The templates provide the structure, an outline, and even instructions on what to write, so it feels more like filling in a form than actually writing an article. We found that developers really like this approach and it makes them more willing to write content.

Besides providing a good workflow and all the supporting materials they need, encouraging contributors is essential. Make sure that developers understand that what you need from them as subject matter experts is the information in any shape or form that they are comfortable to provide. We are highly flexible with our approach. If contributors are not inclined toward writing, they can choose to record a quick screencast where they demonstrate the tutorial, or they can describe the process in Slack or a text file. Based on this input, a technical writer will then craft a tutorial using our template. We always explain that what they contribute is a draft, someone will proofread it and edit it, so they really don't have to worry about how perfect it is. Once developers feel that they can really just share their thoughts on a topic they are passionate about without anyone judging their English or writing skills, we found that they start contributing more and more.

User Research

Chapter 2, "Foundations," explored the role of user research in developing a documentation site in great detail. User research is a fundamental part of documentation development that you can use in all phases of the process. Using the most fitting tools and methodologies, user research can help you gain insights to solve problems large and small. You can get to know your audience, identify their needs, test content and structure, improve all aspects of your documentation, and ensure accessibility.

When you have an active community, organizing user research activities is quite straightforward. Specify the goal and method of the research, which helps you define what type of participants you will need. You can then announce that you are looking for participants on various channels that your community members frequently use. You often don't need a lot of people – we've conducted many successful user research rounds with five to ten people that provided valuable insights to help us move forward.

We found that it's helpful to share the results of each user research initiative or project with your community. For larger changes, we usually present the problem we wanted to solve, the research results, and the improvements based on the results in a live video conference session that we also record. This way, users can react immediately but can also watch the recording later and discuss it on other channels. For smaller changes, we share the results in our regular status reports.

We add a summary of each research on our documentation site. Each research summary has the same outline:

- **Title** that summarizes the goal of the research and conveys whether the research is *ongoing* or *finished*.

- **Date** of the research; we usually add the month and year.

- **Goal** of the research that can include what sparked the need for the research and what we expect to achieve with it.

- **Method** that includes the type of user research method and the number and types of participants.

- **Results** that explain in detail what insights we gained from the research, what we have created based on them (e.g., an affinity map), and what we identified that will help us move forward. If more in-depth analysis is available, we link to it among the results.

Based on our experience, community members appreciate learning about the reasons for changes and knowing about what you are working on behind the scenes, while you can benefit from getting feedback on everything you are planning or doing.

Contributor Experience

To serve a diverse, highly motivated, and active community and provide everything they need to contribute to your documentation, you'll have to think about contributor experience first.

As a starting point, think about **entry points for different types of contributors**. Make it easy to get involved for all segments of your target audience, offer different ways to contribute both regarding the time contributors have to put in and the skill level they need. How will they provide feedback? How can they add or update content? How can they participate in user research?

Always **acknowledge and reward contributors** for their contributions to create a positive contributor experience and encourage ongoing participation. We thank all of our contributors and display them on our GitHub repository's README page and on our contributors page. We always highlight the role our community plays in the success of our documentation, and we encourage community members to share their use cases on our documentation site and in live video conferences.

Develop an editorial workflow that works for internal and external contributors, and ensure that contributors get quick and precise feedback.

Well-organized documentation with a clear structure like specific topic types organized into different sections and categories helps contributors specify the content they would like to provide feedback on or find the place for the content they would like to contribute.

Make sure it's easy for contributors to get on board: add a **Contributor Guide** that is easy to find. Test if your docs site search displays the Contributor Guide among search results for relevant keywords and conduct user research to learn where potential contributors would look for it. The Contributor Guide should be brief but comprehensive. You could start with including the following:

- Information on how to give feedback

- A step-by-step tutorial on how to update existing content and submit new content

- A link to the Style Guide and a description of what the contributor will find there

- A link to the templates and a short description of what they are used for

- A way to get in touch with the documentation team

Based on feedback from your contributors, you can adjust and improve your Contributor Guide just like any other part of your documentation.

Communication

It's important to provide various communication channels to share news and engage in conversations with your community because it enables everyone to choose the channel they feel most comfortable with.

All throughout the process of developing and maintaining your documentation, you need ways for sharing information with your users.

You can share news of new features, improvements, and fixes to your product in **release notes**. Feel free to use the release note template from Chapter 4, "Content Production," and adjust it according to your needs.

Release notes share what you've done; **road maps** show what you are planning to do. Road maps typically include an outline of goals, priorities, and milestones for the next couple of months to a year or longer. As you include planned features, you can include your plans for your documentation alongside them, or even better, have a separate road map for your docs based on the needs and tasks that you identified. Experiment with the level of detail and how far into the future you are willing to commit, and always ask your community for feedback.

We found that regularly sharing **status reports** is a great way to keep our community updated on what we've achieved, what we are working on, and what we are planning for the near future. Our status reports also include calls for contribution and research participation, and the results and analysis of UX research. We share a short description and links to our publications, podcasts we participated in, invitation to webinars and conferences, recordings of conference talks, and anything else that our community might be interested in. Status reports also include release notes that we added since the publication of the last status report. We publish the status reports on our blog and share them on our social channels. Subscribers can get the status reports in an email newsletter, too.

When we started developing our documentation, we published status reports weekly to keep everyone in the loop about what was going on. Later, we switched to biweekly, and now we publish them when we have enough topics to share, every month or so.

For having conversations, a **real-time chat or forum** can be a great solution. One of our main communication channels is dedicated Slack channels, where community members ask questions, share ideas, and get to know our team members and each other. Based on their feedback, we see that community members find it very helpful to be able to directly communicate with us and each other: they can share what they've learned, plan their development in sync with our road map and each other's projects, and allocate their resources according to what's going on in the business and the wider community. We share status reports, release notes, webinar recordings, and any other news on our Slack channel, where community members are quick to share and discuss any thoughts they have related to what we shared. This communication channel feeds our documentation site with the most sought-after topics.

For real-time, face-to-face conversations, you can have **video conferences or webinars** where community members and your team share news, hold presentations, demo features, and discuss future plans. Our team and community members are distributed over different continents, so we try to accommodate participants in different time zones by rotating the time of this event so that everyone has the chance to participate. We also share the recording of each meeting.

If you have a **community site**, it can provide a question-and-answer interface similar to Stack Overflow, or a forum. These platforms enable you to track the questions that most interest your community.

Your **public GitHub repository** can become an important channel for communication as well where community members can open issues, or discuss reported issues or pull requests.

These examples show how you can utilize all channels where your community members interact to gain valuable insights for your documentation. Try out and experiment with different communication channels to find the ones that best fit your needs, and adjust them as your documentation and community grow and develop.

Community

Working together with your UX researchers, community managers, and other team members, you can leverage the power of your product's community for your documentation and build your own community of documentation contributors. Your documentation team can also support community building by learning about your audience, conducting user research, communicating with users, and providing the materials they need to adopt and use your product.

Through the frequent use of documentation and many interactions with your users, your docs and your documentation team members can help set the tone for how your community members communicate with each other. Many processes that enable contribution to your documentation like reviews also provide the framework for community members to interact and collaborate. You can help write and adjust the community guidelines, a set of rules that aims to ensure that you build a safe, inclusive, and welcoming community. The community guidelines typically include the following:

- The expected behavior of community members, like being friendly, patient, respectful, and considerate.

- The tone, language, and conduct for all communication within the community, be it virtual or in person (you might want to list the channels where these rules apply). This part usually includes rules against bullying, hate speech, and harassment.

- Content guidelines that specify what kind of content is allowed and not allowed on community channels, for example, providing rules for self or company promotions, but also for explicit content or spam.

- What to do if you've encountered a violation of the rules in the community.

- Moderation policies that describe how moderators enforce the rules and the consequences for community members who violate them.

Although the code of conduct or community guidelines are a necessary and helpful tool, your community members will be looking to your team members and other active members of your community to know what behavior is welcome and what behavior is not accepted in your community. Be prepared that your community leaders and all members of your team who communicate with community members will inevitably become responsible to model and enforce the rules you created.

Summary

This chapter demonstrated how, thanks to the active involvement of your community, you can focus your attention where you can provide the most value and iteratively build great quality developer documentation. It discussed the following:

- The many different ways your community members can contribute to your documentation, and went into more detail on providing feedback, contributing content, and participating in user research

- What constitutes a great contributor experience

- How you can utilize different communication channels to gain valuable insights for your documentation

- The role your documentation team can play in building a community and fostering a community culture

Now that I have touched upon building a welcoming and inclusive community, let's explore how to ensure that your documentation, which is a crucial resource for users who are learning about and using your product, is both accessible and inclusive.

CHAPTER 7

Accessibility and Inclusion

I have mentioned accessibility throughout this book in connection with user research, the Docs-as-Code approach, reviews, and the documentation style guide – this chapter delves deeper into accessibility and inclusiveness to help you provide people with varying abilities, backgrounds, and circumstances the chance to engage with and make meaningful contributions to your developer documentation.

Accessibility ensures that people with disabilities or impairments (including visual, auditory, cognitive, and motor impairments) can use digital products and services efficiently. **Inclusiveness** ensures that individuals from diverse backgrounds and various circumstances have the opportunity to actively participate and derive benefits from the products, services, and information provided.

Often, when the topics of accessibility and inclusiveness are discussed, various justifications are presented, highlighting the benefits they can bring to businesses. I will also include these arguments as they can help you convince stakeholders to invest in accessibility. Still, I hope that for more and more companies, prioritizing and investing in accessibility and inclusiveness becomes the norm, driven by a genuine commitment to equality and fairness, rather than being contingent on potential business advantages. I acknowledge that businesses operate with limited resources and must be mindful of how they allocate those resources to sustain their

© Diana Lakatos 2023
D. Lakatos, *Crafting Docs for Success*, Design Thinking,
https://doi.org/10.1007/978-1-4842-9594-6_7

operations and drive profitability. However, based on my experience, creating accessible and inclusive developer documentation requires more of a shift in mindset than additional financial investment.

According to the World Health Organization, nearly all individuals will experience **disability** at some point in their lives, either temporarily or permanently. Currently, approximately 1.3 billion people, which accounts for around 16% of the global population, face substantial disabilities. The prevalence of disability is on the rise, largely attributed to population aging and the increasing incidence of noncommunicable diseases. The users of your documentation site may be visually impaired, blind, deaf, or hard of hearing, or could have any other impairment such as a motor impairment that affects how they interact with content online. This means that you have to consider the needs of users who utilize keyboard navigation, magnification, different display settings, screen readers, or voice recognition software.

Neurodiversity encompasses a broad spectrum of variations in brain function and behavioral traits found within the human population. Various studies suggest that approximately 15–20% of the population can be classified as neurodiverse, which includes individuals with dyslexia, dyscalculia, attention-deficit/hyperactivity disorder (ADHD), autism, and others.

What these statistics indicate is that within your team and community, there will be individuals who think, learn, process information, and interact with your documentation differently than others. While these differences can present some unique challenges for your developer documentation, overcoming them will ultimately benefit the entire community. For example, captions benefit everyone in a loud environment or when they need to watch the video without sound, good color contrast is helpful when there is glare on the screen, and a well-defined, logical content structure improves readability and reduces cognitive load for everyone.

Website Accessibility

Where to start when you want to ensure that your developer documentation is accessible and inclusive?

The World Wide Web Consortium (W3C) is an international community and standards organization that develops protocols and guidelines to ensure the long-term growth and accessibility of the World Wide Web. W3C offers internationally recognized standards aimed at promoting web accessibility, which are widely adopted by governments and businesses. One of the most prominent standards is the **Web Content Accessibility Guidelines (WCAG)**[1], which provides comprehensive guidelines for making web content accessible to all users. Another standard you can consult is EN 301 549: European standard for digital accessibility[2]. Ensuring your site's accessibility is a legal requirement in many countries – you can find laws and regulations by country on W3C's Web Accessibility Laws & Policies[3] page.

The four main principles of the WCAG standards state that web content should be

- **Perceivable:** Presented in a way that users can perceive it using their senses. This includes providing alternative text for images, captions for videos, and clear content structure.

- **Operable:** Users should be able to navigate and interact with web content using a wide range of input methods. This includes making the content keyboard accessible, allowing users to skip repetitive content, and providing understandable and predictable navigation.

---

[1]https://www.w3.org/WAI/standards-guidelines/wcag
[2]https://www.deque.com/en-301-549-compliance/
[3]https://www.w3.org/WAI/policies/

- **Understandable:** Presented in a clear and understandable manner. This involves using plain language, organizing content logically, and providing instructions and error messages that are easy to comprehend.

- **Robust:** Web content should be developed using technologies that are compatible with a variety of user agents, including assistive technologies. This ensures that the content remains accessible even as technology evolves.

The WCAG standards include detailed guidelines and success criteria that you can use as a starting point to ensure that your documentation is designed and developed in a manner that prioritizes inclusiveness and accessibility.

There are multiple approaches and tools available to assist you in adhering to accessibility guidelines. For example, following the **Docs-as-Code** approach ensures that accessibility is integrated into the documentation development process:

- Docs as Code fosters **collaboration** between developers, technical writers, designers, and other team members, allowing them to work together to ensure accessibility is incorporated from the outset.

- By using continuous integration and delivery practices, Docs as Code enables automated **accessibility and inclusive language testing** tools to be integrated into the development process, allowing for accessibility issues to be identified and fixed early on.

- **Version control** systems used in Docs as Code allow for accessibility improvements to be tracked and reviewed over time, ensuring ongoing accessibility enhancements.

- Docs as Code encourages a **structured and consistent** approach to documentation, which can be designed to incorporate accessibility features such as clear headings, alternative text descriptions for images, and semantic markup. By using semantic HTML correctly and exclusively, assistive technologies (like screen readers) can convey information to their users by following the semantic structure. In addition to providing and ensuring a consistent structure, semantic HTML ensures that web browsers apply default accessibility features for specific HTML elements. For example, buttons get keyboard accessibility (can be navigated to and clicked using the keyboard).

- Docs as Code enables documentation to be easily repurposed and reused, which can help ensure accessibility improvements are consistent across an entire organization's documentation.

Many **tools, plug-ins, and checklists** are available **for designers** to maximize the accessibility of their designs. At platformOS, we use Figma's Able accessibility plug-in[4]. We follow the rules for foreground and background color contrast[5], font size, and graphical objects (like icons, form fields, etc.) to ensure that our developer documentation site conforms with WCAG AAA[6].

---

[4]https://www.figma.com/community/plugin/734693888346260052/
Able-%E2%80%93-Friction-free-accessibility
[5]https://webaim.org/resources/contrastchecker/
[6]https://www.w3.org/WAI/WCAG2AAA-Conformance.html

As many essential requirements for web accessibility are technical, your **development team** should be familiar with Key WCAG Success Criteria for Developers[7] such as associating a label with every form control, ensuring that all interactive elements are keyboard accessible, establishing the proper reading order, and many others to ensure that all of the technical foundations for accessibility are incorporated into the code of your developer documentation site.

Accessibility checkers allow you to regularly test for accessibility and ensure that the site complies with all accessibility requirements. They use a combination of automated checks and predefined accessibility guidelines to evaluate the accessibility of the code and content of a web page. As the checker performs the automated checks, it scans the code, compares the code and content against a set of accessibility guidelines, and tests for common accessibility issues, such as the contrast ratio of the background and foreground colors, missing alternative text for images, improper heading structure, or inaccessible form elements. Finally, the checker generates a report that highlights accessibility issues it found and ways to fix them. As these tools assess your site, they also calculate an accessibility score, allowing you to monitor the impact of your improvements on the overall accessibility of your documentation.

We regularly test for accessibility to ensure that the platformOS Documentation complies with all accessibility requirements. We usually use multiple tools to catch the most issues we can. Figures 7-1, 7-2, and 7-3 show the accessibility audit results of the platformOS Documentation in Google Lighthouse[8], WAVE Web Accessibility Evaluation Tools[9], and AChecker (Web Accessibility Checker)[10], respectively.

---

[7]https://wcag.com/developers
[8]https://developer.chrome.com/docs/lighthouse/overview/
[9]https://wave.webaim.org/
[10]https://achecker.achecks.ca/checker/index.php

Accessibility

These checks highlight opportunities to improve the accessibility of your web app. Only a subset of accessibility issues can be automatically detected so manual testing is also encouraged.

ADDITIONAL ITEMS TO MANUALLY CHECK (10)   Show

These items address areas which an automated testing tool cannot cover. Learn more in our guide on conducting an accessibility review.

PASSED AUDITS (20)   Hide

- ● [aria-*] attributes match their roles   ⌄
- ● [aria-hidden="true"] is not present on the document <body>   ⌄
- ● [role]s have all required [aria-*] attributes   ⌄
- ● [role] values are valid   ⌄
- ● [aria-*] attributes have valid values   ⌄
- ● [aria-*] attributes are valid and not misspelled   ⌄
- ● Buttons have an accessible name   ⌄
- ● ARIA IDs are unique   ⌄
- ● Image elements have [alt] attributes   ⌄
- ● Form elements have associated labels   ⌄
- ● [user-scalable="no"] is not used in the <meta name="viewport"> element and the [maximum-scale] attribute is not less than 5.   ⌄
- ● [aria-hidden="true"] elements do not contain focusable descendents   ⌄
- ● Background and foreground colors have a sufficient contrast ratio   ⌄
- ● Document has a <title> element   ⌄
- ● <html> element has a [lang] attribute   ⌄
- ● <html> element has a valid value for its [lang] attribute   ⌄
- ● Links have a discernible name   ⌄
- ● Lists contain only <li> elements and script supporting elements (<script> and <template>).   ⌄
- ● List items (<li>) are contained within <ul>, <ol> or <menu> parent elements   ⌄
- ● Heading elements appear in a sequentially-descending order   ⌄

NOT APPLICABLE (24)   Show

Figure 7-1. *Overall accessibility score and passed audits of the platformOS Documentation in Google Lighthouse*

Figure 7-2. *The results of the platformOS Documentation using the WAVE accessibility checker*

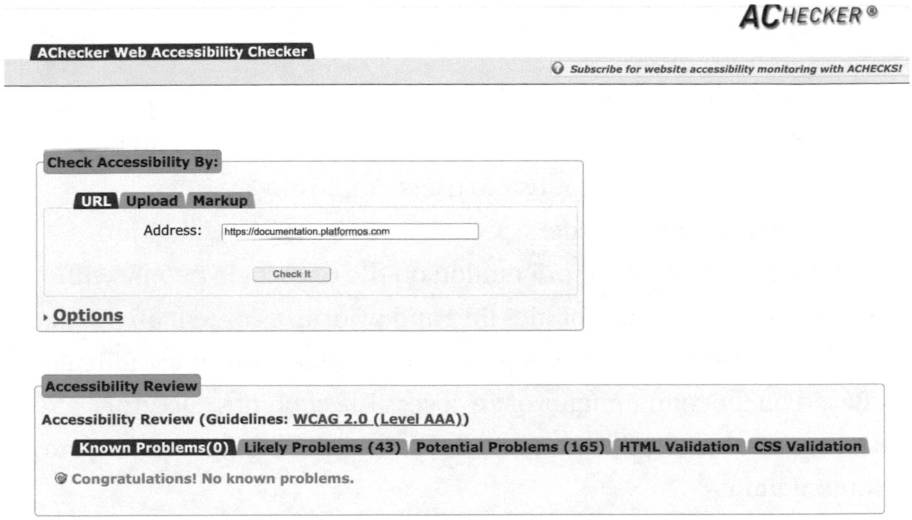

Figure 7-3. *The results of the platformOS Documentation using AChecker, tested against WCAG 2.0 AAA*

Accessibility checkers can identify many common accessibility issues, but as they rely on automated checks, it's always best to include manual testing including assistive technologies, expert evaluation, and user feedback into your accessibility reviews.

Writing for Accessibility

The technical aspects discussed so far serve as the foundation for web accessibility. However, to create a truly accessible website, it is essential to go beyond technical considerations and embrace a mindset of writing for accessibility, which means making deliberate choices during content creation to ensure that information is conveyed effectively and inclusively.

Guidelines for Structuring Content

The code and content structure of your documentation pages plays a crucial role in ensuring accessibility. By using structural elements correctly, you can provide context to users employing assistive technologies like screen readers, provide cues for users with vision impairments that help their orientation on the page, help people with cognitive and learning disabilities find and prioritize content on the page, and help keyboard users browse pages and page sections more efficiently.

Based on the requirements of an accessible content structure, there are some basic guidelines to follow when writing content for your documentation.

- Use headers for structuring your content: The Markdown format you write in is translated into semantic HTML to help screen readers navigate through the content. Use headers as described in the style guide and follow the provided templates to ensure consistency. Never skip a header level for styling reasons.

- Improve readability by using concise language, writing short paragraphs, and using lists where applicable.

- Use alternative text for images and icons. Keep in mind that screen readers read this text out loud.

  - If the image serves a function as part of the documentation, describe the image in detail. Users should receive the same information from the alt text that they would receive if they saw the image.

  - Include the data for charts or graphs in the alt text.

- When you use screenshots to show what the user has to do, the alt text shouldn't repeat the information already described in text.

- Decorative images don't need alt text – it would only be a distraction. When a screen reader encounters an image with null alt text, it skips over the image without acknowledging its existence. On the other hand, if an image lacks an alt attribute, the screen reader will announce the file name of the image. This could potentially be a significant disruption for individuals who rely on screen-reading technology.

- If you insert an image, pay attention to the contrast ratio, image quality, and its size in kilobytes. The smaller the image, the more accessible it is because images with smaller file sizes load faster, reducing wait times for users, particularly those with slower Internet connections.

- Use informative link text: To help keyboard navigation, add the information into the link text. For example, instead of writing "learn more" or "click here", write the topic title.

- If you're using videos, make sure to also provide the information in text. Not everyone finds videos easy to use. Also, many people like to speed up videos to save time, or read the closed captions if they find it easier to learn by reading than by listening.

Tip   Feel free to paste these instructions into your documentation style guide or use them as a starting point to write your own.

A logical content structure enhances the overall user experience for all users of your documentation, as clear and organized content with well-defined headings, logical flow, and easy navigation makes it easier for everyone to find and consume information efficiently and makes your website easier to crawl for search engines, ensuring that the data is indexed correctly, which leads to better search results.

Guidelines for Accessible and Inclusive Language

Using accessible and inclusive language is an important part of promoting accessibility. Language is considered accessible and inclusive when it reflects your users' diversity including, for example, ability, race, gender, or cultural background. By embracing inclusive language, you can enhance the accessibility of your content and demonstrate respect for a diverse audience.

Note   The guidelines I discuss in this section are tailored to developer documentation in English, but most principles could be used for documentation content written in other languages as well.

Here's a short list of guidelines for accessible and inclusive language:

- Use definitions for all terminology: Introduce new concepts by starting with a definition, and add them to the Glossary. Explain acronyms at first use.

- Use technical language: Use the most specific word you can to talk about technical concepts and processes. For example, don't say "take" when you mean "copy," don't say "put" when you mean "install," etc.

- Use gender-neutral pronouns: Avoid gender-specific pronouns such as "he" or "she." Use the second person "you" instead and "they" when necessary.

- Avoid assuming ability: Don't use words that assume an ability the user might not have (e.g., "as you can see" implies the user has a capacity for vision). Avoid directional language, for example, "blue button" or "button below the headline."

- Don't perpetuate racism, bias, and harm: Replace terms like "blacklist" and "whitelist" with terms like "allowed" or "blocked." Replace "native" with "built-in." The Inclusive Naming Initiative[11] offers open-sourced word lists categorized in tiers, which can serve as a helpful guide for teams aiming to implement inclusive language.

  Note: If the application you describe includes these terms, you have to use them in the documentation for clarity and consistency.

- Avoid metaphors and colloquialisms. This makes writing more straightforward and easier to understand for people whose first language isn't English and for neurodivergent users, who may interpret the text literally.

Tip   Feel free to paste these instructions into your documentation style guide or use them as a starting point to write your own.

---

[11]https://inclusivenaming.org

When contemplating word choice, grammar, and style for your documentation content, getting familiar with the principles of plain language and Simplified Technical English (STE) can be immensely beneficial. Even if you don't have to adhere to the guidelines of these approaches, becoming acquainted with them can greatly contribute to the clarity, conciseness, and overall understandability of your writing.

Plain Language

According to the Plain Writing Act of 2010[12], plain language is defined as

> *Writing that is clear, concise, well-organized, and follows other best practices appropriate to the subject or field and intended audience.*

Plain language is closely connected to the audience of your content: it's language that helps the audience quickly find the information they are looking for, understand it the first time they read or hear it, and effectively apply the knowledge to accomplish their intended tasks.

Note   These criteria are in line with some of the requirements for information quality, which I explore further in Chapter 10, "Measures of Success."

Plain language focuses on using clear and straightforward language that is free from unnecessary jargon, complex terms, and convoluted sentence structures. It requires you to follow guidelines that are best practices for documentation sites as well such as using active voice and present tense, organizing information, being concise and consistent, and using examples. It also emphasizes that you should conduct user research to get to know your audience, test your assumptions, test the content you created, and adjust it based on user feedback.

---

[12]https://www.govinfo.gov/app/details/PLAW-111publ274

By following plain language principles, you can ensure that your documentation is accessible to a wider audience, including those with limited language proficiency or cognitive challenges. It promotes comprehension and reduces ambiguity, allowing readers to grasp the information more easily.

While not specifically targeted at documentarians, plainlanguage. gov[13] collects a lot of useful resources like templates, checklists, examples, books, articles, and many more that you can use to understand and apply plain language principles in your documentation work.

Simplified Technical English

The **ASD-STE100 specification**[14], usually referred to as Simplified Technical English or STE, is a controlled language intended to be used in technical documentation. It aims to enhance clarity and comprehension by utilizing a controlled vocabulary and standard grammar rules. The specification provides the following:

- A **set of grammar rules** for procedural and descriptive writing. For example, STE rules require you to only use approved words (listed in the dictionary) with their meaning as specified in the dictionary, use only approved forms of verbs, not use passive voice in procedures, and use the active voice as much as possible in descriptive text. It also specifies the maximum number of words in sentences and the maximum number of sentences in a paragraph, along with rules for noun clusters and verb structures, and many others.

---

[13]https://www.plainlanguage.gov
[14]https://www.asd-ste100.org/

- A **dictionary** of approved words with their approved meaning and examples of approved and not approved uses.

STE is primarily used in industries where precise and unambiguous communication is of utmost importance, such as aerospace (where it originates from), defense, and other technical fields. It has been adopted in various sectors that require clear and standardized communication, including engineering, manufacturing, and transportation. Even if you don't have a specific requirement to follow the STE specification for your developer documentation project, exploring STE can still help you by enhancing your understanding of clear and concise technical communication, providing insights into standardizing terminology, and reducing ambiguity in your documentation. Applying only selected STE guidelines can also improve the overall clarity and readability of your documentation.

Prioritizing accessible and inclusive writing in your developer documentation ensures that the information you provide is comprehensible and usable by a diverse range of readers, regardless of their abilities or backgrounds. By removing barriers and accommodating different needs, you promote inclusivity, foster equal access to knowledge, and enhance the overall user experience.

Accessibility Reviews

Regular accessibility reviews are crucial for both improving existing documentation and building new documentation because they help you identify and fix problems, stay up to date with accessibility best practices, ensure ongoing compliance with standards and regulations, and improve the overall user experience.

Depending on the resources available to you, you can include the following activities in an accessibility review:

- Conduct accessibility audits using automated tools like **accessibility checkers and inclusive language linters**. These can also be incorporated into your CI/CD process.

- Perform manual testing by utilizing **assistive technologies** such as screen readers or keyboard navigation.

- Involve users with disabilities in **usability testing** and gathering valuable feedback on accessibility barriers they may encounter.

- Consult **accessibility experts** and involve them in testing.

- Hire accessibility experts to conduct a detailed **accessibility audit** of your website. Such audits usually provide a detailed report of areas on your site that pass and fail accessibility standards, feedback on how to improve areas that failed, and an accessibility statement after the audit is complete and the fixes have been implemented.

Tip   If you want to educate yourself and your team about different aspects of accessibility, look for courses and workshops, such as the free courses Introduction to Web Accessibility[15] by the W3C, Learn Accessibility[16] by web.dev, and Web Accessibility by Google[17], or paid

---

[15]https://www.classcentral.com/course/edx-introduction-to-web-accessibility-17252

[16]https://www.classcentral.com/course/independent-learn-accessibility-137866

[17]https://www.classcentral.com/course/udacity-web-accessibility-6531

courses and certifications like the courses by The A11Y Collective[18] for designers, developers, and writers. Great books on the topic of accessibility and inclusiveness include *Accessibility for Everyone*[19] by Laura Kalbag and *Inclusive Design for a Digital World: Designing with Accessibility in Mind*[20] by Regine M. Gilbert.

Summary

This chapter discussed how to develop and refine your documentation to provide an accessible and inclusive experience for all users, including

- What accessibility and inclusiveness are and why they matter

- How to ensure that your developer documentation is accessible and inclusive

- How to write accessible and inclusive documentation content

- The components of accessibility reviews

- Resources and tools for designers, developers, and writers

I hope this chapter has provided valuable insights that inspire you to take a proactive approach toward accessibility and inclusiveness, thus contributing to a more accessible Internet, one documentation at a time.

---

[18]https://www.a11y-collective.com/courses-overview/
[19]https://abookapart.com/products/accessibility-for-everyone
[20]https://www.amazon.com/Inclusive-Design-Digital-World-Accessibility/dp/148425015X

CHAPTER 8

Sustainability

Based on total ICT emissions from the article "How to stop data centres from gobbling up the world's electricity[1]" compared with Carbon emission by country[2], if the Internet was a country, it would be in the top ten of largest polluters.

When you use the Internet, your device, data transferred through the Web, the servers where the data is hosted, and hardware production to create and replace the servers, wires, and devices all consume energy.

According to Mike Hazas, a researcher at Lancaster University (UK)[3], the amount of electricity required to run our digital lives is one-tenth of the electricity used globally in total, which is a similar level to that of air conditioning used around the world. From the point of view of our carbon footprint, that's about 3% of global emissions, which is a similar level to that of the airline industry.

What's even more alarming is that the electricity consumption and carbon emissions from our digital lives are on a sharp increase. For example, according to Ericsson's traffic measurement reports, mobile phone data traffic has doubled every two to three years, and broadband and business Internet traffic is also constantly on the rise.

There are many ways to decrease the carbon footprint of your digital lives as an individual, for example, turning off your routers when you leave

---

[1]https://www.nature.com/articles/d41586-018-06610-y
[2]https://en.wikipedia.org/wiki/List_of_countries_by_carbon_dioxide_emissions
[3]https://www.youtube.com/watch?v=QYRy8ghVlOU

© Diana Lakatos 2023
D. Lakatos, *Crafting Docs for Success*, Design Thinking,
https://doi.org/10.1007/978-1-4842-9594-6_8

for a couple of days or more, or not running streaming services in the background. Learn about the environmental impact of web development and how to make the Internet more sustainable to be able to make conscious choices as you're building your developer documentation site.

What Would a Sustainable Internet Look Like?

The Sustainable Web Manifesto[4] describes the requirements for a sustainable Internet.

- **Clean:** The services you provide and services you use should be powered by renewable energy.

- **Efficient:** The products and services you provide should use the least amount of energy and material resources possible.

- **Open:** The products and services you provide should be accessible, allow for the open exchange of information, and allow users to control their data.

- **Honest:** The products and services you provide should not mislead or exploit users in their design or content.

- **Regenerative:** The products and services you provide should support an economy that nourishes the people and the planet.

- **Resilient:** The products and services you provide will function in the times and places where people need them most.

---

[4]https://www.sustainablewebmanifesto.com/

Based on these guidelines, you can understand the factors that you need to keep in mind when developing a sustainable website. By signing the manifesto, you can declare your commitment to building a greener web.

What Makes a Website Sustainable?

The less energy a website uses, and the more that energy is sourced from sustainable means, the more sustainable the website is. There are many ways to enhance the energy efficiency of your website. From strategic planning to continuous tweaks and adjustments, you have a wide range of improvements you can implement.

There are some website checkers that you can use to analyze various sustainability aspects of your documentation site. To compare your site's carbon footprint to that of other websites, use the Website Carbon Calculator[5]. To calculate the environmental impact of your site, use Beacon[6] or Ecograder[7] that utilizes CO2.js from The Green Web Foundation and Google Lighthouse's page metrics to rate the sustainability of your site. Tools like these usually provide some insights on why your site got the result it did and advice on what you can do to improve your site's sustainability.

Figure 8-1 shows that based on the Website Carbon Calculator, the platformOS Documentation runs on sustainable energy and is cleaner than 96% of websites tested. Figure 8-2 shows the results of our documentation site on Ecograder, while Figure 8-3 shows the results on Beacon.

---

[5]https://www.websitecarbon.com/
[6]https://digitalbeacon.co/
[7]https://ecograder.com/

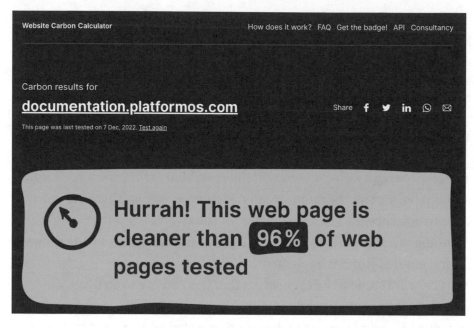

Figure 8-1. *The result of the platformOS Documentation on the Website Carbon Calculator*

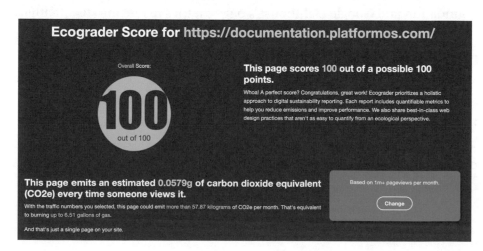

Figure 8-2. *The result of the platformOS Documentation on Ecograder*

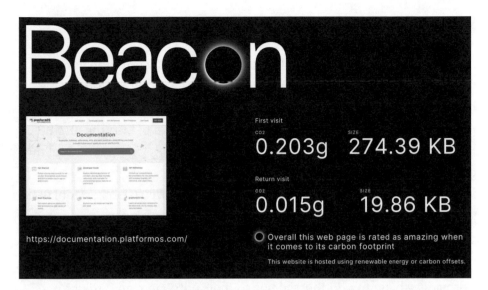

Figure 8-3. *The result of the platformOS Documentation on Beacon*

Many of the best practices you can follow are just as beneficial for your users as the planet, for example, achieving the best possible performance or providing the best user experience tailored to the needs of your audience.

These are the main areas you can focus on to improve a site's sustainability:

- Hosting

- Performance

- Image management

- Video management

- Fonts

- Web caching

- User experience

- Content management

- Search engine optimization

- Third-party tools

Hosting

Making your website sustainable starts with planning how and where you will host it. To reduce your carbon footprint, you should preferably host your website in the Cloud on a Green Web Server. Green hosting providers run websites on renewable energy instead of burning fossil fuels to power their servers, data centers, and cooling systems and follow environmentally conscious practices.

The Green Web Foundation provides a Green Web Checker[8] tool that you can use to verify that your website runs on renewable energy.

Note   The Green Web Foundation is a work in progress and hosting providers have to add themselves to their database, so it might not include all current green hosting companies in the world.

Figure 8-4 shows the results of the platformOS Documentation on the Green Web Checker. It displays the hosting provider if it has been added to the database and some links to supporting evidence for the hosting provider's claims. Our documentation is hosted on Oracle Cloud behind Cloudflare.

---

[8]https://www.thegreenwebfoundation.org/green-web-check/

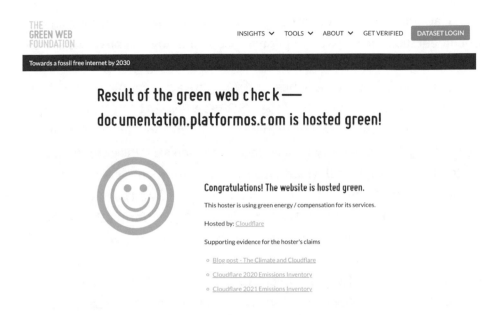

Figure 8-4. *Results of the platformOS Documentation on the Green Web Checker*

To find a green hosting provider, you can check the Hosting Directory of the Green Web Foundation[9] that lists submitted green hosting providers by country, or go with one of the carbon-neutral website hosts that run only on renewable energy like the Google Cloud Platform[10].

Performance

Website performance, specifically speed and page load times, is directly linked to sustainability. Faster-loading websites require less server resources and have shorter data transmission times, therefore consuming less energy.

---

[9]https://www.thegreenwebfoundation.org/directory/
[10]https://cloud.google.com/

In addition to this direct impact on sustainability, it is crucial for your documentation site to have exceptional speed for many other reasons as well. Great performance ensures that visitors remain engaged on your site and enjoy an optimal user experience, and your site achieves high rankings in search results. According to the Google/SOASTA Research 2017, as the page load time goes from one second to three seconds, the probability of bounce increases by 32%, and the more page load time increases, the grimmer the outlook; for example, if the load time increases from one second to five seconds, the probability of bounce increases by 90% and so on.

This demonstrates that investing in improving performance yields multiple benefits – a more sustainable website being only one of them.

To measure the performance of your site, you can use tools like Google Lighthouse[11] (which I already mentioned in relation to measuring accessibility) or PageSpeed Insights[12]. Both report on the performance of your site on desktop and mobile devices and offer suggestions to improve your performance metrics. It's useful to learn how these tools calculate the performance score, why it might fluctuate, and how weighted metrics have an effect on your performance score. Lighthouse also offers a scoring calculator that lets you experiment with different values for metrics like First Contentful Paint (FCP), Speed Index (SI), Largest Contentful Paint (LCP), Total Blocking Time (TBT), and Cumulative Layout Shift (CLS) to learn how they influence your overall performance score and to understand what thresholds to aim for to achieve a certain overall score. Conduct tests across multiple pages and carefully define the desired outcomes you aim to achieve based on the specific characteristics of each type of page.

Figure 8-5 shows the PageSpeed Insights scores for the home page of the platformOS Documentation. From the start, we recognized the significance of performance and consistently made adjustments to achieve these results.

---

[11]https://developer.chrome.com/docs/lighthouse/overview/
[12]https://pagespeed.web.dev/

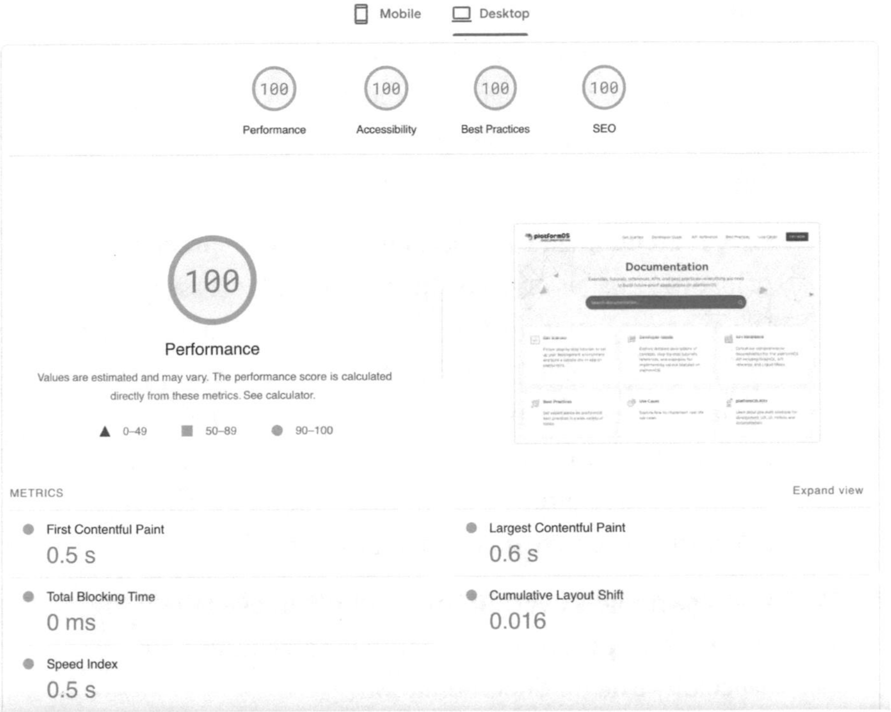

Figure 8-5. *The PageSpeed Insights results of the platformOS Documentation*

Image Management

Images play a substantial role in the overall size of your website, and their hosting and downloading processes contribute significantly to your site's energy consumption. Therefore, you can improve the sustainability of your website by optimizing image management.

- **Make images smaller:** Reduce the size of images by lowering image resolution and image quality.

- **Choose the most efficient format for the information presented:** Find the image format that works best for the content of the image, for example, JPG for photos, PNG for images with transparency, and GIF and CSS Sprites for frequently used images like icons.

- **Lazy load images:** Lazy loading refers to the practice of loading images on your site only when necessary. When a user first visits a page, the content that is immediately visible "above the fold" loads instantly, but the remaining content is loaded progressively as the user scrolls down the page. If a user does not scroll all the way to the bottom, the images and other media in that part of your site do not need to be loaded.

- **Use less images overall:** Only include images that serve a clear purpose. This is true for all content but especially true for documentation.

Video Management

While embedding videos on your website might add code snippets that can affect page load times, when implemented properly, videos should not have a significant impact on your site's performance.

To ensure that video integration won't affect load times, start with identifying the current load times to establish a baseline. Then, decide if you would like to host videos or use an external solution like YouTube or Wistia. Self-hosted videos provide benefits like full control over the content and the appearance of video but, in general, have been shown to take longer to load than external videos. Media players of streaming services are designed to be embedded on websites and are optimized for both mobile and desktop use. If you use YouTube, you can embed the thumbnail image and only load the video when a user clicks on the media player.

Similar to images, carefully consider the purpose and value of videos before including them, and ensure that they are beneficial and valuable to your audience.

Fonts

The different types of fonts you can use in your documentation site's design have different impacts on its sustainability:

- **System fonts** like Arial or Times New Roman are available as a default on all types of devices. They require the least amount of energy to load, as they are installed on local computers, but can be limiting to the design.

- **Web fonts** are hosted online; therefore, they become available on all devices that load them. They expand your design options but can affect page load times. The Google Fonts library offers a wide range of free and open source typefaces to choose from.

- You can also purchase a font and turn it into a **DIY web font**. How DIY web fonts affect page load times depends entirely on how they are optimized.

In general, you can minimize server load time by being thoughtful about how you use fonts; for example, you can use web fonts for headers and a system font for body copy, or limit the number of web fonts you use overall.

Web Caching

Caching means that you store shared page elements closer to the user to improve website performance and reduce data transfer. It helps reduce server load and enhances the browsing experience. To plan a sustainable web caching strategy, consider the frequency of content changes: the duration of caching should be determined based on the specific content to make sure that what you display is accurate with the smallest environmental impact possible.

User Experience

The more time users spend on your site loading page after page trying to find information they need, the more energy your site consumes (and the more frustrated your users become). This is why providing good user experience is so beneficial for the sustainability of your site. Make sure that users quickly find what they are looking for by planning and adjusting your site navigation based on the findings of user research and by making sure your search gives users the results they expected.

Content Management

A content delivery network (CDN) is a geographically distributed group of servers that caches content close to end users and helps quick transfer of assets needed to load website content, like HTML, JavaScript files, images, videos, and so on. Using a CDN contributes to sustainability by improving page load times, optimizing data transfers, and reducing the load on origin servers.

Search Engine Optimization

When you optimize your documentation site for search engines, users interested in your content can quickly find the information they are looking for without having to click on multiple sites and pages. Additionally, by reducing page load times and making your website more environmentally friendly, you can improve its search engine ranking.

Third-Party Tools

Using third-party tools like website analytics or trackers for user behavior can slow your site down and have a significant impact on sustainability, so be very intentional with any third-party tools you use. Are they really needed? Which tool is the most sustainable for the purpose you would use it for? How long do you need to use them to get the data you need? For the platformOS Documentation, we use Plausible Analytics, a lightweight Google Analytics alternative that fully complies with GDPR, CCPA, and PECR regulations. We only utilize other tools for the briefest periods necessary for specific user research initiatives.

There are many other ways to improve the sustainability of your website. Make sure to educate your team about sustainability and continuously experiment with ways to make your documentation more environmentally friendly.

Tip   I recommend starting with the books *Sustainable Web Design*[13] by Tom Greenwood and *Designing for Sustainability: A Guide to Building Greener Digital Products and Services*[14] by Tim Frick and online resources like the Sustainable Web Manifesto[15] and thegreenwebfoundation.org[16].

Summary

This chapter focused on making your developer documentation more sustainable and discussed topics like

- Why sustainability matters

- What a sustainable Internet would look like

- What makes a website sustainable

- Ways to reduce the environmental impact of your documentation site

I trust that this chapter has demonstrated the advantages of implementing sustainability best practices, benefiting both your users and the planet. I hope it has also inspired you to explore ways for enhancing the sustainability of your developer documentation.

---

[13]https://abookapart.com/products/sustainable-web-design/

[14]https://www.amazon.com.au/Designing-Sustainability-Building-Products-Services-ebook/dp/B01KW8O848

[15]https://www.sustainablewebmanifesto.com/

[16]https://www.thegreenwebfoundation.org/

CHAPTER 9

Team

It will require the collective effort of multiple team members to accomplish all the tasks described in this book. This chapter delves into the distinctive contributions that each member of your documentation team can make, ways in which you can help them bring their best to your project, and the available resources that can enhance everyone's understanding of developing developer documentation.

The Members of Your Documentation Team

The members and size of your documentation team may vary widely based on your company size, the product you develop, or the phase of the process you are in. Regardless of these factors, you'll need the contribution of key roles that are essential for the success of your documentation.

First of all, you need a company leadership who understands the value of great developer documentation and can recognize your **docs as a product** that demands careful strategy, significant time investment, ample resources, and adequate funding. Make sure to communicate your progress and regularly share user feedback so that your leadership can be aware of the ongoing value your team is delivering.

© Diana Lakatos 2023
D. Lakatos, *Crafting Docs for Success*, Design Thinking,
https://doi.org/10.1007/978-1-4842-9594-6_9

Tip   You can use the list from the section "Documentation As a Product" of Chapter 1, "Approaches," as a starting point to collect arguments for convincing your leadership about the value developer documentation can bring to the business. You can use the roles explained in this chapter to start thinking about how you'll assemble your documentation team.

Now, let's delve into the different key roles in your team and what they bring to your project. It's worth noting that many of these roles can be sourced from larger teams and don't necessarily have to focus solely on documentation. In fact, the responsibilities of various roles can often be merged and consolidated into a single role. For instance, in smaller teams, the information architect and interaction designer responsibilities may be combined with either the UX researcher or the UX designer role. Similarly, the tasks typically assigned to a UX writer often involve collaboration between UX practitioners and technical writers.

Documentation Lead

The leader of your documentation team can go by many names: Director of Documentation, Documentation Strategist, Head of Documentation, and so on. As we've established that your documentation is a product, they can also be considered the product owner of your documentation, but some companies have a separate product owner, too. This role is highly strategic.

The documentation lead has a vision and road map for your developer documentation in sync with the needs of your target audience and the company's goals. They help establish and manage processes, standards, and guidelines and work closely with technical writers to manage and improve your editorial workflow, style guide, and templates for different types of documentation content.

They incorporate documentation best practices and ensure accessibility, inclusiveness, and sustainability.

Together with UX researchers, they manage getting user feedback and work with developers to improve the documentation based on the feedback received.

Being aware of the company's short-term and long-term goals, the documentation lead also manages and prioritizes tasks for the team.

They can work with marketing to promote your documentation through various publications, conferences, or awards.

The documentation lead is usually responsible for assembling the documentation team, providing education for team members, and managing collaboration with other teams.

What the documentation lead needs to do their work well is information and feedback, both from the leadership regarding company goals and business strategy and from documentation team members about processes, tools, and all other aspects of the work they are doing.

Technical Writer/Editor

Technical writers are responsible for creating and maintaining the content of your developer documentation. They collaborate with SMEs (subject matter experts) to research, organize, and write content and ensure the accuracy and consistency of the documentation. They may also be involved in designing the structure and layout of the documentation, choosing the appropriate tools and technologies for the project, and managing and fine-tuning the editorial workflow.

Most often, technical writers review and edit documentation topics submitted by internal or external contributors. If you have technical editors on your team, you can divide writing and review tasks between writers and editors.

They contribute the most to the style guide, create templates for content, and suggest improvements.

Besides documentation topics, you will probably find that they will be asked to write all kinds of technical content, like articles, webinar transcripts, presentations, and so on.

To help your technical writers bring their best to the project, develop processes and use tools that allow them to focus on writing.

UX Researcher

The UX researcher's role focuses on the development and execution of research studies and usability tests that inform the design and development of user experiences for your developer documentation.

This includes defining and optimizing research processes to ensure that they are efficient, effective, and aligned with best practices. They will need to stay up to date with the latest research methodologies and techniques, continually learning and adapting to new approaches as needed.

In addition to managing research processes, they oversee research tool management, ensuring that your team has access to the necessary tools and technologies to conduct research studies. This may involve researching and evaluating new tools, managing licenses, and ensuring that tools are up to date and properly configured to meet the needs of your team.

They also create documentation for research practices, including research templates and other resources that enable your team to work efficiently and effectively.

When you share your research findings with your community, UX researchers can write research summaries and hold presentations about the methods, findings, and work done based on the results.

As part of their role, they prioritize research work based on the needs of the business, advocating for the importance of research in decision-making processes.

As this book showed, UX researchers should be involved in developing a developer documentation site from the very beginning to get to know all stakeholders, be able to reveal missing information, and plan research accordingly. User input is critical to the success of your project – UX researchers drive evidence-based decision-making and inform the design and development of your documentation site.

Information Architect

The information architect (IA) is involved in developing and optimizing the information architecture of your documentation, ensuring that users can easily find the information they need. They work closely with UX researchers and designers to understand user needs, behavior, and expectations and translate these insights into effective information structures.

Involve the information architect early on so that they can tell you what information is needed from stakeholders. Based on research results, the information architect can plan the information architecture, which is later validated by internal and external stakeholders.

Interaction Designer

The interaction designer role involves designing and optimizing the way users interact with your developer documentation. This includes defining and improving interaction design processes and staying up to date with industry trends and best practices. For interactive developer documentation, it is beneficial to have someone who understands common features like "Try it out" from the Swagger UI output commonly seen in REST API websites. An interaction designer with specialty knowledge for developer documentation websites can be valuable in ensuring seamless user experiences. Additionally, when dealing with complex code examples within the documentation, the interaction designer should have a deep empathy for developers and possess an understanding of their specific needs and use cases.

UX Writer

UX writers create the text that appears on buttons, forms, menus, and other interface elements. They also write microcopy, such as error messages, tooltips, and notifications.

UX Designer

Working closely with the UX researcher and the information architect, UX designers develop user flows, wireframes, and prototypes to create an intuitive and seamless user experience.

Involve the UX designer latest when sharing the research results so that they can learn about the user needs, and keep them involved in the information architecture phase so that they are aware of the structure and logic of the planned documentation site. Later, the UX researcher supports the testing and iterating of screen flows.

UI Designer

Based on the wireframes and prototypes, the UI designer creates visually appealing interfaces for your documentation that include layouts, fonts, icons, buttons, and other graphical elements. They make sure that the style of your documentation is in sync with your brand and the design adheres to accessibility guidelines. Furthermore, when integrating the documentation within the product's user interface or when linking to specific sections, the UI designer should also be involved in maintaining visual alignment and interaction patterns and ensuring a cohesive look and feel. This collaboration helps to seamlessly integrate the documentation elements with the overall product experience.

To help UI designers on your project, make sure to share requirements early and (if possible) provide them with the final content.

Developers

Developers working on your documentation can contribute in two distinct ways: by developing, adjusting, and improving the documentation site and by providing information to technical writers as subject matter experts.

As they are working on your product just like your target audience, you can involve the developers of your product and documentation in any phase of the project to conduct some inhouse user research, get ideas and feedback, or brainstorm together. If you make sure to validate the results with real members of your target audience later, such quick research rounds can really help propel your documentation development forward.

To help developers working on your documentation site, give them as much information about the requirements and then as much autonomy to find a technical solution for the challenges as you can. Involve them in planning, developing, and testing the tools and processes for the editorial workflow and for different features of the site.

Developers as SMEs can contribute drafts, outlines, code examples, screencasts, diagrams, and videos. As discussed before, you can help them by accepting their contributions in different formats they are comfortable with as your capacity to turn them into topics allows.

Some developers also like to hold presentations and live coding sessions, or explain features of your documentation site to users through video conferences. It's important to record all such events, including sprint demos, and transform them into useful materials for your documentation.

Quality Assurance

The QA team is responsible for reviewing, testing, and validating the documentation to identify any issues or inconsistencies before it is published. They set up automated tests; do manual testing on the site; check the accuracy and correctness of code examples; report identified issues, inconsistencies, or errors using your issue management tool; and verify that the reported issues have been resolved.

Along with content reviewers, the QA team plays an important role in ensuring that your developer documentation meets high-quality standards and provides accurate and reliable information in a user-friendly way.

Automation and DocOps

DocOps, short for Documentation Operations, is the practice of integrating documentation processes and workflows within the broader context of software development and operations. It plays an important role in establishing an efficient Docs-as-Code developer documentation site, particularly when combined with a CI/CD workflow. The responsibility for DocOps and automation is commonly shared among different roles and teams, with developers and testers playing a central role in its successful implementation.

Project Management

Depending on the size of the business and the resources dedicated to the documentation, the project can have its own **product manager**, **project manager**, or **scrum master** (if you follow the scrum methodology), while in other teams, the responsibilities of these roles are divided between the documentation lead and other members of the team.

Regardless of the different positions you have on your team, you have to make sure to have someone who assigns tasks, tracks progress, and facilitates communication within the team. Having a smooth process helps everyone on the team have a good understanding of priorities and deadlines and uninterrupted time to work.

As I mentioned regarding some of these roles, not all of them might be present in a developer documentation project at all times. The resources the business can allocate for the documentation depend on a lot of factors like the financial situation of the company, other projects team members have to work on, available talent, and so on. If you work in a smaller company or a startup, team members will probably have to fulfill the responsibilities of multiple roles, and there might be times when you really have to juggle with the capacities of team members to be able to move your documentation forward. In such cases, my recommendation is to work with what you have and never stop improving your docs. If all of your developers have to be moved to an urgent client project, work on the content, prepare conference talks, look for ways to promote your docs – do anything but standing still. And while you are filling in the gaps, keep advocating for the importance of your documentation to eventually build a solid team that you can always count on.

Educating Your Team Members

To educate and keep your team members informed about topics related to developer documentation, events and communities offer valuable opportunities for learning, networking, and staying updated on the latest trends and best practices in the field.

Some notable **communities and conferences** for professionals working on developer documentation:

- **Write the Docs[1]:** Write the Docs has an active online community where you can engage in discussions, share resources, and seek advice on documentation-related topics. Write the Docs is also the name of a series of conferences held in different locations worldwide, including online, that focuses on all aspects of documentation and technical writing.

- **API The Docs[2]:** API The Docs events serve technologists involved in the documentation, developer relations, marketing, and UX of API programs: members of API teams who want to create great developer experiences and, ultimately, developer success.

- **DevRelCon[3]:** DevRelCon is a series of conferences aimed at sharing and levelling up knowledge of developer relations including topics related to developer experience, community, and developer marketing.

- **ISTC[4] and TCUK[5]:** The Institute of Scientific and Technical Communicators (ISTC) is the largest UK body representing information development professionals. TCUK, or Technical Communication UK, is the ISTC's annual conference for everyone involved in writing, editing, illustrating, delivering, and publishing technical information.

---

[1] https://www.writethedocs.org/
[2] https://apithedocs.org/
[3] https://developerrelations.com/devrelcon
[4] https://istc.org.uk/
[5] https://istc.org.uk/tcuk/

- **STC[6] and STC Summit[7]:** The Society for Technical Communication is the world's largest and oldest professional association dedicated to the advancement of the field of technical communication. The STC Summit is an annual conference that gathers technical communicators from various industries. It covers a wide range of topics related to documentation, content creation, and user experience.

All throughout this book, I mentioned some resources for learning about developer documentation and other topics related to technical writing; here's a list of my recommendations:

- *Docs Like Code*[8] book and docslikecode.com[9] by Anne Gentle

- *Docs for Developers: An Engineer's Field Guide to Technical Writing*[10] by Jared Bhatti, Sarah Corleissen, Jen Lambourne, David Nunez, and Heidi Waterhouse

- *The Product is Docs: Writing technical documentation in a product development group*[11] by Christopher Gales[12] and the Splunk Documentation Team[13]

---

[6]https://www.stc.org/

[7]https://summit.stc.org/

[8]https://www.amazon.com/Docs-Like-Code-Anne-Gentle/dp/1387081322

[9]https://www.docslikecode.com/

[10]https://link.springer.com/book/10.1007/978-1-4842-7217-6

[11]https://www.amazon.com/Product-Docs-technical-documentation-development-ebook/dp/B085KHTV95

[12]https://www.amazon.com/s/ref=dp_byline_sr_ebooks_1?ie=UTF8&field-author=Christopher+Gales&text=Christopher+Gales&sort=relevancerank&search-alias=digital-text

[13]https://www.amazon.com/s/ref=dp_byline_sr_ebooks_2?ie=UTF8&field-author=Splunk+Documentation+Team&text=Splunk+Documentation+Team&sort=relevancerank&search-alias=digital-text

- Documenting APIs: A guide for technical writers and engineers[14] course and idratherbewriting.com[15] by Tom Johnson

- Docsbydesign.com[16] by Robert Watson

- Courses about API technical writing by Peter Gruenbaum on Udemy[17]

Encourage your team members to get actively involved in **open source communities** as one of the best ways to get inspired by processes, learn about tools, and get real-life experience is by contributing to open source projects. I know I'll forever be grateful to the Drupal community. A wonderful opportunity for gaining practical experience is the Google Season of Docs[18] program. This program offers support to open source projects, helping them improve their documentation. Simultaneously, it provides professional technical writers with a valuable opportunity to gain experience in open source communities.

Summary

In this chapter, I outlined the various roles required for your documentation team and explained their responsibilities. I also discussed how to support the work of each role and how to educate your team members about topics related to developer documentation.

Having covered the steps of developing your developer documentation and forming your team, it is now time to delve into the metrics that you can employ to ensure the high quality of the documentation you are creating.

---

[14]https://idratherbewriting.com/learnapidoc/
[15]https://idratherbewriting.com/
[16]https://docsbydesign.com/
[17]https://www.udemy.com/user/petergruenbaum/
[18]https://developers.google.com/season-of-docs

CHAPTER 10

Measures of Success

While setting objectives, prioritizing tasks, and crafting your documentation, crucial questions emerge: How can you assess your success? How can you evaluate the tangible and intangible outcomes of your efforts? How can you determine the quality and effectiveness of your documentation?

Success in developer documentation is not a one-time achievement but a continuous process of improvement and adaptation. Your documentation evolves in sync with product enhancements, user research findings, changes in user needs, and shifts in industry standards. Your goal should not be to reach an elusive state of perfect documentation, but rather to establish robust, resilient, adaptable systems that empower you to refine and enhance your docs in a practical and efficient manner.

So how can you identify the measures of success in the context of developer documentation? Let's delve into some metrics and indicators that can help you gauge the effectiveness of your initiatives and steer your future strategies.

Documentation Quality

To start creating good quality documentation, you'll have to gain an understanding of the key metrics that define documentation quality, including the quality of information contained in your documentation and the features of the website where your users can interact with your docs.

© Diana Lakatos 2023
D. Lakatos, *Crafting Docs for Success*, Design Thinking,
https://doi.org/10.1007/978-1-4842-9594-6_10

Information Quality

Information quality refers to the characteristics and attributes of information that determine its value to the intended audience. As previous research has shown, the definition and criteria for information quality may not be universally applicable.

Note   Numerous resources are available that delve into the criteria for information quality. In "Beyond Accuracy: What Documentation Quality Means to Readers[1]," Yoel Strimling explores previous research that has aimed to define information quality and discovers a diverse array of definitions. Other sources you can get insights from include Tom Johnson's Quality Checklist for API Documentation[2], the research titled "Beyond Accuracy: What Data Quality Means to Data Consumers[3]" by Richard Y. Wang and Diane M. Strong, and the book *Developing Quality Technical Information: A Handbook for Writers and Editors*[4] by Michelle Carey, Moira McFadden Lanyi, Deirdre Longo, Eric Radzinski, Shannon Rouiller, and Elizabeth Wilde. Delving into these resources can provide a comprehensive understanding of information quality, but for now, let's focus on the key criteria that have been consistently highlighted across multiple sources.

---

[1] https://www.researchgate.net/publication/331088095_Beyond_Accuracy_What_Documentation_Quality_Means_to_Readers

[2] https://idratherbewriting.com/learnapidoc/docapis_quality_checklist.html

[3] http://mitiq.mit.edu/Documents/Publications/TDQMpub/14_Beyond_Accuracy.pdf

[4] https://www.oreilly.com/library/view/developing-quality-technical/9780133119046/

Accuracy is one of the primary aspects commonly discussed in information quality research. Your documentation is considered accurate if all the information provided including descriptions, diagrams, screenshots, videos, and code examples are factually correct, reliable, up to date, and free from errors. It also means that your documentation is consistent and does not include any contradictory information. If you share example code in separate repositories, they should be considered part of the documentation, so test and verify all code examples to ensure that they work as intended and align with the explanations in the documentation.

Regular reviews, frequent updates, and validation by subject matter experts can help maintain the integrity of the information. Update or remove outdated information and display the date of the last update on each documentation page. Mark deprecated features and redirect the user to information on how to replace the deprecated functionality.

Building and maintaining your developer documentation is an ongoing process. Your documentation undergoes continuous changes as you add new topics, update, or remove existing ones to align with product features, and make adjustments to the design, content, or functionality of your documentation site based on user feedback. While you may perceive your developer documentation as never being truly finished, you should strive for **completeness** by including all necessary information to effectively address user needs. For example, when documenting procedures, make sure that all steps are included in the right order and no steps are missing, and provide the necessary prerequisites and next steps. Your API reference documentation should adhere to industry standards and be comprehensive; reference of parameters should include the name, description, type, values (default, min, max), required/optional usage, and constraints. Striking a balance between completeness and **conciseness** is essential. While completeness ensures that users have all the information they need, it's equally important that the documentation doesn't overwhelm users with too much information. Regular user research and feedback can provide valuable insights into which parts of the documentation are helpful and which are not, and it can also reveal what information might be missing. User testing can show whether users can successfully use the product by relying solely on the documentation. Templates for different content types aid contributors in ensuring no information is overlooked by providing the outline for a complete topic.

Readability refers to the ease with which a reader can understand and navigate the information presented, and as such, it directly impacts the effectiveness and usability of developer documentation. Your goal is to present complex technical information in a manner that's not just accurate and complete, but also **understandable** and digestible, ensuring developers can quickly comprehend the material and apply it effectively. Use clear, straightforward language, define technical terms, and add them to the glossary. Be aware of sentence structure: short, concise sentences and paragraphs are generally easier to understand than long, complex ones.

Clarity in the writing helps avoid misunderstandings, while a clear information architecture aids users in finding the information they are looking for. **Findability** of information is key to developer documentation, so make sure that your site is indexed in general search engines and test that searches for important keywords return relevant results. Your documentation should also have an effective site search feature, ideally incorporating built-in analytics. Site search analysis involves closely examining how visitors interact with the search function on your website. This can include behaviors like keyword searches and search suggestion clicks. The insights gained from this analysis can be used to enhance the user experience. For instance, if you notice that your users are searching for certain keywords that return no results, you may need to develop new content that covers these topics or better optimize existing content to match these keywords. This ensures that your users can find the information they're looking for, improving their overall experience on your documentation site. On the other hand, if there are keywords that are frequently searched for on your site and have corresponding documentation topics, you could focus on making this content easier to find. You can also gain a better understanding of the terminology your users use and make sure to include that terminology in your documentation topics.

Note   The platformOS Documentation uses DocSearch[5] by Algolia, a customizable and fast open source search solution developed for developer documentation sites.

The information you provide has to be **relevant**, directly applicable, and meaningful to the user's context or needs. Your docs should address real-world use cases and scenarios that developers are likely to encounter when using your product. Irrelevant information can overwhelm the user, cause confusion, and make it harder to find the necessary information. Relevance is also connected to delivering information in a **timely** manner; for example, the documentation of new features should be published at the same time the new features are released. To be able to produce relevant documentation, you need to develop a deep understanding of the intended audience – this is one of the reasons why I strongly emphasized the importance of user research throughout this book.

Documentation Site

Your users primarily interact with your documentation through your website or developer portal, while contributors also participate via a version control system, such as Git, facilitated by platforms like GitHub. This implies that their overall user experience is shaped not only by the quality of information in your documentation but also by the features and characteristics of your website and the efficiency of your editorial workflow.

---

[5]https://docsearch.algolia.com/

Numerous aspects explored in this book aim to cultivate an environment that enables your target audience to effectively utilize your documentation. Now, let's delve into the metrics that can assist you in crafting the optimal experience for your users.

Activity

By adopting a Docs-as-Code approach, you can effectively monitor all modifications made to your documentation, track the number of contributors, assess the frequency of updates, and trace everything down to the smallest commit.

Platforms like GitHub or GitLab provide insights and analytics about a repository's activity. For example, GitHub Insights, as shown in Figure 10-1, offers a visual representation of the repository's history, showcasing information such as contributions, issue activity, and pull request activity.

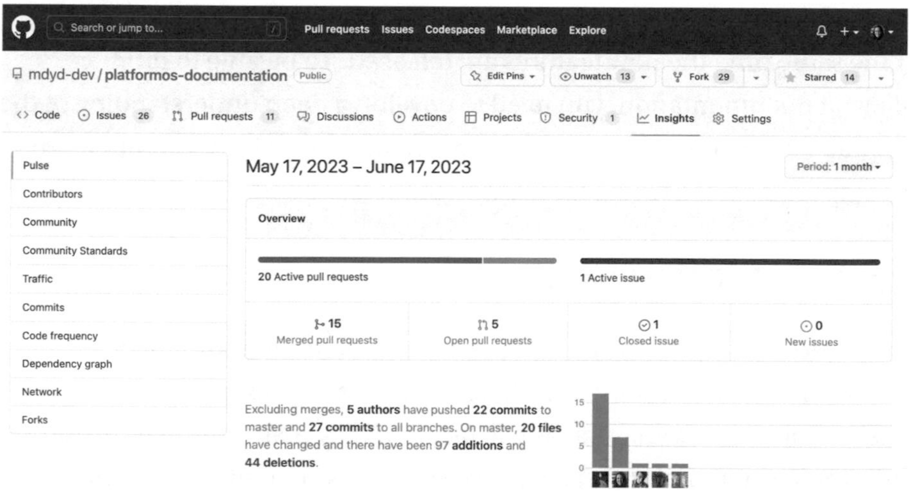

Figure 10-1. *The GitHub Insights overview (Pulse) page of the platformOS Documentation's GitHub repository*

By examining and exploring the provided data, you can gain a comprehensive understanding of the project's development patterns, community involvement, and activity level; identify recurring trends; and monitor the repository's progress over time.

While metrics like number of commits, files modified, or issues closed are easily accessible and even presented in a user-friendly format, it is important to be mindful not to utilize them to measure your team's productivity or how much value they bring to the business. Instead, collaborate with your users to figure out what they need, improve your documentation based on the insights you gained, and validate that your users are satisfied with the changes. This qualitative approach serves as a more effective indicator of your documentation team's contributions to the business.

Linters

In addition to providing access to detailed repository data, a Docs-as-Code approach is well suited for incorporating automated tests and linters into your deployment workflow. For example, you can test for broken links, check for grammar and spelling errors, catch offenses to inclusive writing and suggest alternatives, or measure the readability score of your content.

Some automation tools worth checking out are

- vale.sh[6] prose linter

- Alex.js[7] prose linter for inclusive writing

- Acrolinx[8] content optimization software

- EkLine.io[9] process automation software for standardization, optimization, and analytics

---

[6]https://vale.sh/
[7]https://alexjs.com/
[8]https://www.acrolinx.com/
[9]https://ekline.io/

You can also use linters to utilize grammar and spelling checkers like the Hemingway App[10] or Grammarly[11].

Besides being useful tools to improve the quality of your content, linters can provide various metrics, depending on their focus and functionality. Language linters such as Acrolinx or Grammarly typically evaluate texts based on factors like grammar, spelling, punctuation, clarity, readability, engagement, delivery, and style. They use sophisticated algorithms and databases of rules to analyze your text, providing scores and recommendations. Grammarly provides an overall score on a scale of 0 to 100, representing the quality of your writing compared to other Grammarly users in similar contexts. This score tells you the percentage of all content that Grammarly analyzes, which your text ranks better than. For example, a Grammarly score of 80 means your content ranks better than 80% of all the content Grammarly analyzes.

The Acrolinx score measures your content's quality based on guidelines you set in the Acrolinx platform, also ranging from 0 to 100. An Acrolinx score over 79 is considered excellent.

Linters can be used to gauge how much your content has improved while you are refining it. As you enhance your content, the overall scores, like the Grammarly and Acrolinx scores we discussed, should increase, while reported issues in checkers, such as those with inclusive language, should decrease.

Website Metrics and Analytics

In previous chapters on accessibility and sustainability, I have introduced tools for measuring different aspects of your website, such as performance and compliance with accessibility standards. Still, there's one more tool left to discuss – site analytics.

---

[10]http://www.hemingwayapp.com/
[11]https://app.grammarly.com/

Site analytics tools like Google Analytics[12] or Plausible.io[13] provide various types of data about visitors, traffic, device and browser information, page views, and bounce rates that offer insights into website performance and user behavior.

Site analytics can provide insights into your users, including their geographical location, device usage, and behavior on your website. You can understand where they are from, which pages they visit most frequently, where they click, and how much time they spend on each page. However, it's important to note that site analytics alone do not provide a complete understanding of their intentions, needs, or the overall experience they had on your site. To gain deeper insights into user intent and satisfaction, it is necessary to combine site analytics with other methods such as user feedback, user research, and usability testing.

The analytics process starts by defining the problem or goal, followed by obtaining and preparing the necessary data. The data is then analyzed, visualized if needed, and used to describe user behavior and diagnose potential issues. Based on the findings, you can create a plan for improvement and may also use predictive analytics to anticipate future trends.

The documentation lead, along with technical writers and UX researchers, often defines the problem or goal and proposes enhancements. Data analysts or scientists, if available, manage data preparation, analysis, and visualization. In the absence of these specialists, UX researchers may assume these duties. The documentation lead can aid in defining objectives, while UX professionals might help with interpreting data and analyzing user behavior. However, the particular roles can fluctuate based on the team's structure and resources.

---

[12]https://analytics.google.com/
[13]https://plausible.io/

Defining the goal and verifying that the information you gain from analytics helps you attain insights to achieve the goal are critical and help you avoid getting caught up in easily measurable vanity metrics. Vanity metrics are data points that might appear impressive but don't offer actionable insights or contribute directly to the improvement of your documentation. Examples include the total number of visitors, page views, or bounce rates, which, when taken out of context or viewed without considering long-term trends, don't provide much useful information. Without a clear goal and plan to utilize the data, it's easy to lose the potential gains from the analytics.

Bear in mind that **site analytics data, without context, is not reliable** – you should never rely solely on a single metric. For instance, high bounce rates could suggest that most users find the information they were looking for. Similarly, interpreting time spent on a page can be tricky – do users spend more time on a page because it's helpful, or because it's difficult to understand? Even if you follow the best practice to look at trends and not absolute numbers, it is recommended to only use site analytics as supplementary information to support your decision-making process. It's essential to cross-reference these metrics with other sources of information, such as user feedback or usability studies, to gain a more comprehensive understanding of your users' needs and experiences. Site analytics can provide you with quantitative data, like page views or search terms, but it will not offer the qualitative insights that come from direct user interactions.

Business Value

To assess the value your developer documentation brings to the business, your management may be interested in monitoring the impact of your documentation efforts.

An evident measure is the **reduction in customer support tickets**, as developer documentation plays a crucial role in developer onboarding and education. High-quality documentation can significantly deflect support tickets, leading to a direct reduction in operating costs for the business. By tracking the decline in support tickets over time (always factoring in product growth) and correlating it with the views of documentation topics, you can demonstrate how the documentation contributed to lowering support costs.

From the perspective of your support team, an important aspect of your documentation is its ability to **reduce the time required to locate information and resolve issues**. This can be reflected in the response time to resolve support requests, making it a valuable metric. Ideally, over time, your support team should be able to address most inquiries by referring users to relevant topics in your documentation.

Great documentation can significantly contribute to user satisfaction and **user retention**. As users become proficient with your product by learning from the documentation, they develop a deeper engagement with it. This increase in product competency and subsequent satisfaction often encourages users to continue using your product.

Well-executed **SEO** on your documentation site can significantly **reduce paid marketing costs**. When your relevant and high-quality content naturally appears in search engine results, it attracts organic traffic, reducing your reliance on paid advertising and thus lowering overall marketing costs. Furthermore, organic visitors, finding your content based on their search intent, often engage more effectively than paid traffic.

Developer documentation plays an important role in developer onboarding, education, communication, community engagement, marketing, and support. It provides essential information, fosters self-help, keeps users informed on changes, builds trust, facilitates collaboration, acts as a marketing tool, aids support teams, and forms the basis for developer education initiatives. To comprehensively evaluate the effectiveness and value of developer documentation, it is essential to assess a range of metrics. These include measuring onboarding success, conducting user research, tracking community growth, and evaluating support efficiency. By considering a wide range of metrics, businesses can gain a holistic understanding of the impact of developer documentation efforts.

Success

Throughout this book, I have emphasized the significance of involving your users in the creation and testing of your developer documentation. This emphasis on user involvement is rooted in the understanding that developer documentation is a vital resource that empowers users, enhances their understanding of your product, and enables them to leverage its full potential, which means that **the ultimate measure of success for developer documentation lies in its ability to effectively serve the users of your product**.

Delve into extensive research and draw upon valuable experiences to gain insights into the key elements that define high-quality developer documentation. I hope that the insights I have shared with you in this book will assist you on your journey to craft successful developer documentation.

Summary

This chapter explored various metrics that can bolster your efforts toward enhancing your developer documentation. Key points discussed include the following:

- Identifying the primary criteria frequently associated with information quality

- Exploring how adopting a Docs-as-Code approach can support your objectives by

  - Utilizing data from your version control system

  - Incorporating linters and checkers into your deployment workflow for improved quality control

- Learning how to interpret website analytics effectively to draw reliable insights and inform decision-making

- Measuring the impact of documentation on the business

APPENDIX

Tools and Resources

This appendix serves as a comprehensive inventory of tools and resources that have been referenced throughout the course of this book.

Tools

Docs as Code

- GitHub(https://github.com/)
    - GitHub Actions(https://github.com/features/actions)
    - GitHub Issues(https://github.com/features/issues)
- GitLab(https://about.gitlab.com/)
- Gerrit(https://www.gerritcodereview.com/)
- Bitbucket(https://bitbucket.org/)
- Jenkins(https://www.jenkins.io/)
- Netlify(https://www.netlify.com/)

Content editor

- VS Code(https://code.visualstudio.com/)

© Diana Lakatos 2023
D. Lakatos, *Crafting Docs for Success*, Design Thinking,
https://doi.org/10.1007/978-1-4842-9594-6

Website crawlers

- SEO Spider(https://www.screamingfrog.co.uk/seo-spider/)

- SEMRush(https://www.semrush.com/)

Digital whiteboards

- Miro(https://miro.com/)

- Mural(https://www.mural.co/)

- FigJam(https://www.figma.com/figjam/)

Auto-generated changelog

- release-please(https://github.com/googleapis/release-please)

- auto-changelog(https://github.com/cookpete/auto-changelog)

Static site generators

- Asciidoctor(https://asciidoctor.org/)

- Sphinx(https://www.sphinx-doc.org/en/master/)

- Docusaurus(https://docusaurus.io/)

- Jekyll(https://jekyllrb.com/)

- Hugo(https://gohugo.io/)

- Gatsby(https://www.gatsbyjs.com/)

- MkDocs(https://www.mkdocs.org/)

Documentation hosting platforms

- Read the Docs(https://readthedocs.org/)

- GitBook(https://www.gitbook.com/)

- SwaggerHub(https://swagger.io/tools/ swaggerhub/)

- GitHub Pages(https://pages.github.com/)

- Redocly(https://redocly.com/)

- Stoplight Elements(https://stoplight.io/ open-source/elements)

Wireframing, prototyping

- Balsamiq(https://balsamiq.com/)

- Marvel(https://marvelapp.com/)

- Figma(https://www.figma.com/)

Sustainability

- Website Carbon Calculator (https://www.websitecarbon.com/)

- Beacon(https://digitalbeacon.co/)

- Ecograder(https://ecograder.com/)

- Green Web Checker(https://www. thegreenwebfoundation.org/green-web-check/)

Performance

- Google Lighthouse(https://developer.chrome.com/docs/lighthouse/overview/)

- PageSpeed Insights(https://pagespeed.web.dev/)

Accessibility

- Google Lighthouse(https://developer.chrome.com/docs/lighthouse/overview/)

- WAVE Web Accessibility Evaluation Tools (https://wave.webaim.org/)

- AChecker (Web Accessibility Checker) (https://achecker.achecks.ca/checker/index.php)

- WebAIM Contrast Checker (https://webaim.org/resources/contrastchecker/)

- Figma's Able accessibility plug-in(https://www.figma.com/community/plugin/734693888346260052/Able-%E2%80%93-Friction-free-accessibility)

Search

- DocSearch(https://docsearch.algolia.com/) by Algolia

Linters, automation tools for writing

- vale.sh(https://vale.sh/)

- Alex.js(https://alexjs.com/)

- Acrolinx(https://www.acrolinx.com/)

- EkLine.io(https://ekline.io/)

- Hemingway App(http://www.hemingwayapp.com/)

- Grammarly(https://app.grammarly.com/)

Specifications, references

- Darwin Information Typing Architecture (DITA)
  (http://docs.oasis-open.org/dita/dita/v1.3/
  dita-v1.3-part0-overview.html)

Markup languages

- Markdown(https://www.markdownguide.org/)

- GitHub Flavored Markdown
  (https://github.github.com/gfm/)

- Leanpub Flavoured Markdown
  (https://leanpub.com/lfm/read)

- CommonMark(https://commonmark.org/)

- reStructuredText
  (https://docutils.sourceforge.io/rst.html)

- AsciiDoc(https://asciidoc.org/)

- MDX(https://mdxjs.com/)

Style guides

- AP Stylebook(https://www.apstylebook.com/)

- The Chicago Manual of Style
  (https://www.chicagomanualofstyle.org/home.html)

- Apple Style Guide(https://support.apple.com/
  en-gb/guide/applestyleguide/welcome/web)

- Microsoft Writing Style Guide(https://learn.
  microsoft.com/en-us/style-guide/welcome/)

- Google Developer Documentation Style Guide
  (https://developers.google.com/style)

- Red Hat Technical Writing Style Guide
  (https://stylepedia.net/)

API reference

- OpenAPI Specification
  (https://swagger.io/resources/open-api/)

Version control

- Conventional Commits
  (https://www.conventionalcommits.org/)

Accessibility

- WCAG AAA(https://www.w3.org/WAI/WCAG2AAA-
  Conformance.html)

- EN 301 549: European standard for digital accessibility
  (https://www.deque.com/en-301-549-compliance/)

- Web Accessibility Laws & Policies
  (https://www.w3.org/WAI/policies/)

Inclusion

- Plain Writing Act of 2010(https://www.govinfo.gov/
  app/details/PLAW-111publ274)

- ASD-STE100 specification
  (https://www.asd-ste100.org/)

- Inclusive Naming Initiative
  (https://inclusivenaming.org)

Books, articles, courses

Design Thinking

- *The Design Thinking Playbook*(https://www.amazon.
  de/-/en/Michael-Lewrick/dp/1119467470) by
  Michael Lewrick, Patrick Link, and Larry Leifer

- Apress Design Thinking series
  (https://www.springer.com/series/15933)

- Articles on Design Thinking by the Interaction Design
  Foundation(https://www.interaction-design.org/)

Docs as Code

- *Docs Like Code*(https://www.docslikecode.com/book/)
  by Anne Gentle

Developer documentation

- *Docs for Developers: An Engineer's Field Guide to Technical Writing*(https://link.springer.com/book/10.1007/978-1-4842-7217-6) by Jared Bhatti, Sarah Corleissen, Jen Lambourne, David Nunez, and Heidi Waterhouse

- *The Product is Docs: Writing technical documentation in a product development group*(https://www.amazon.com/Product-Docs-technical-documentation-development-ebook/dp/B085KHTV95) by Christopher Gales(https://www.amazon.com/s/ref=dp_byline_sr_ebooks_1?ie=UTF8&field-author=Christopher+Gales&text=Christopher+Gales&sort=relevancerank&search-alias=digital-text) and the Splunk Documentation Team(https://www.amazon.com/s/ref=dp_byline_sr_ebooks_2?ie=UTF8&field-author=Splunk+Documentation+Team&text=Splunk+Documentation+Team&sort=relevancerank&search-alias=digital-text)

User experience research

- *Universal Methods of Design – 125 Ways to Research Complex Problems, Develop Innovative Ideas, and Design Effective Solutions*(https://www.amazon.com/Universal-Methods-Design-Expanded-Revised/dp/1631597485) by Bella Martin and Bruce Hanington

- *Just Enough Research*(https://abookapart.com/products/just-enough-research) by Erica Hall

Version control

- *Beginning Git and GitHub*(https://www.amazon.com/ Beginning Git-GitHub-Comprehensive-Management/ dp/1484253124) by Mariot Tsitoara

Sustainability

- *Sustainable Web Design*(https://abookapart. com/products/sustainable-web-design/) by Tom Greenwood

- *Designing for Sustainability: A Guide to Building Greener Digital Products and Services*(https:// www.amazon.com.au/Designing-Sustainability- Building-Products-Services-ebook/dp/B01KW80848) by Tim Frick

- Sustainable Web Manifesto (https://www.sustainablewebmanifesto.com/)

- The Green Web Foundation (https://www.thegreenwebfoundation.org/)

Accessibility

- Key WCAG Success Criteria for Developers (https://wcag.com/developers)

- Introduction to Web Accessibility(https://www. classcentral.com/course/edx-introduction-to- web-accessibility-17252) by the W3C

- Learn Accessibility(https://www.classcentral.com/course/independent-learn-accessibility-137866) by web.dev

- Web Accessibility by Google(https://www.classcentral.com/course/udacity-web-accessibility-6531)

- Courses by The A11Y Collective(https://www.a11y-collective.com/courses-overview/)

- *Accessibility for Everyone*(https://abookapart.com/products/accessibility-for-everyone) by Laura Kalbag

- *Inclusive Design for a Digital World: Designing with Accessibility in Mind*(https://www.amazon.com/Inclusive-Design-Digital-World-Accessibility/dp/148425015X) by Regine M. Gilbert

API documentation, technical writing

- Documenting APIs: A guide for technical writers and engineers(https://idratherbewriting.com/learnapidoc/) by Tom Johnson

- Docs by Design(https://docsbydesign.com/) by Robert Watson

- Courses about API technical writing by Peter Gruenbaum on Udemy(https://www.udemy.com/user/petergruenbaum/)

Metrics

- Beyond Accuracy: What Documentation Quality Means to Readers(https://www.researchgate.net/publication/331088095_Beyond_Accuracy_What_Documentation_Quality_Means_to_Readers) by Yoel Strimling

- Quality Checklist for API Documentation(https://idratherbewriting.com/learnapidoc/docapis_quality_checklist.html) by Tom Johnson

- Beyond Accuracy: What Data Quality Means to Data Consumers(http://mitiq.mit.edu/Documents/Publications/TDQMpub/14_Beyond_Accuracy.pdf) by Richard Y. Wang and Diane M. Strong

- Developing Quality Technical Information: A Handbook for Writers and Editors(https://www.oreilly.com/library/view/developing-quality-technical/9780133119046/) by Michelle Carey, Moira McFadden Lanyi, Deirdre Longo, Eric Radzinski, Shannon Rouiller, and Elizabeth Wilde

Community, conferences

- Write the Docs(https://www.writethedocs.org/)
- API The Docs(https://apithedocs.org/)
- DevRelCon(https://developerrelations.com/devrelcon)
- ISTC(https://istc.org.uk/) and TCUK (https://istc.org.uk/tcuk/)

- STC(https://www.stc.org/) and STC Summit (https://summit.stc.org/)

- Google Season of Docs(https://developers.google.com/season-of-docs)

Research papers

- Clarke, S. (2007) What is an end user software engineer?(https://drops.dagstuhl.de/opus/volltexte/2007/1080/) – Dagstuhl Seminar Proceedings, Schloss Dagstuhl – Leibniz-Zentrum für Informatik

- Watson, R. B. (2015) The effect of visual design and information content on readers' assessments of API reference topics(https://digital.lib.washington.edu/researchworks/handle/1773/33466) (doctoral dissertation)

- Meng, M., Steinhardt, S., Schubert, A. (2019) How Developers Use API Documentation: An Observation Study(https://www.researchgate.net/publication/335456576_How_developers_use_API_documentation_an_observation_study) – Communication Design Quarterly (January 29, 2019)

Award programs

- DevPortal Awards(https://devportalawards.org/)

- DevRel Awards(https://devrelawards.com/)

- UK Technical Communication Awards(https://istc.org.uk/homepage/professional-development-and-recognition/uk-technical-communication-awards/)

Index

D

Printed in the United States
by Baker & Taylor Publisher Services